Joe & Andy

THROUGH DIFFERENT EYES

The Grand Social Experiment
That is Columbia, Maryland

Because diversity matters!

NANCY SELIG AMSDEN

1/13/17

Published and distributed by
Transformation Publishing
www.transformation-publishing.com

ISBN 978-1-60166-048-0

CONTENTS

This book is dedicated to my parents,
Marc and Toby Selig.

ACKNOWLEDGEMENTS

Barbara Kellner, Columbia Association and the Columbia Archives for their information, the letter from Mr. Rouse, his picture, and their efforts to preserve all that makes Columbia so special.

Bob Murphy for all of the pictures and news clips that helped me to illustrate the story.

Natalie Rivera, editor and publisher at Transformation Publishing, without whom this book would never have happened. To being a big part of my inspiration to write the book, and being a great daughter and human being. I love you!

To my parents, Marc and Toby Selig (in loving memory) who set the example for me on what it means to truly honor diversity. They were the model Columbia citizens. Their devotion to the City of Columbia was evident throughout all their years in Columbia. Their continuing passion for honoring diversity and embracing people for who they were on the inside, not on the outside, was a real influence in the community. This was not only in their living, but in their passing as well. The testimony of the community was so profound for me and was the initial seed that was planted from which this book has grown. I love and miss you, Mom and Dad!

To my brothers Sam and Matt and my sister Rachel who brought to my life so much joy and provided for a life full of diverse and interesting experiences.

And mostly to James Rouse, a visionary whose passion for humankind helped to create one of the most unique, accepting, ecumenical and ethnically diverse communities in the world. I will be forever grateful for the opportunity to have participated in his "grand social experiment", and for the impact that has had on my life.

The many fellow Columbians who impacted my life and provided insight and support during the writing of this book.

In Appreciation of the Following Contributors

Bill Lawrence	Ken Carlson
Brian Rich	Laura Moss
Charles S. Rowley Jr.	Linda (Green) Schreiber
Chaya Kaplan	Michele Carberry-Fujikawa
Claudia (Wehdeking) Friend	Natalie (Amsden) Rivera
Collette Smith	Robin Brodkin
Debbie (Sprinsock) Nix	Sari Hendrixson Chapman
Donna Craig	Scott Kramer
Gayle Harvey DeBaun	Sue (Sprinsock) Smith
Julie Hunter	Sue Hallman
Karen Bradley Ehler	

PREFACE

I moved back to Florida from Maryland in the fall of 2013. I had a feeling like there was something I was supposed to do, and Florida was where I needed to be. I kept struggling with the desire to find my purpose, yet I didn't really know where to begin. I had my children young (first at 20 and second at 25) and for the next 25 years (give or take a year) my purpose was to raise my girls to be balanced, caring, loving, intelligent and independent young women.

My husband (now ex) Steve and I always strived to bring our daughters up in an environment where they would know acceptance and unconditional love — where their strengths would be rewarded, their individuality acknowledged and they would always know that they were loved for all that they are, not what we wanted them to be. We let them explore their world. We did not have a lot of rules, anticipation of raising a doctor and a lawyer or a list of punishments. We didn't "spank them" or ground them for every "wrongdoing" (or ever, for that matter), but we did set boundaries. For us, it was all about setting the expectation and letting them make their own choices. In retrospect, we did a pretty damn good job, if I do say so myself. While writing this book and reflecting on my history, I could see clearly from where my progressive parenting style had emerged.

So, at 44, I became an empty-nester. The path before me was unknown. With child rearing having been our primary purpose and now behind us, Steve and I discovered that what we wanted for our future was not the same. Shortly after our move to Florida late in 2006, my husband of 27 years and I went our separate ways. Both of us needed to forge our own paths. We never had the opportunity to discover our own paths, being that we traveled down the same path, together, from a very young age. (No regrets!) When our marriage was winding down, I remember my husband telling me that he was "holding me back." I didn't understand what he was talking about at the time, but shortly after we split, I began to understand. I have been learning more each day since, about the woman that I am, have been and will become. He was right...

Before I delve into my new-found purpose, let me tell you a little about myself, and Steve's, background. This information should help to set the stage for the book—the backdrop for my ultimate purpose... I was born to a Jewish mom and dad in the little town of Amityville, New York (yup—the horror). My mom was an artist and my dad an engineer. Around my first birthday, we moved to Newport News, Virginia where my dad had a new job working on a nuclear submarine. This town was not a very hospitable place for a young Jewish couple with very left leanings. Within a matter of only a few weeks, the neighbors had burned a cross on our front yard. (More on that later.)

My family packed up, my dad got a new job at Goddard Space Flight Center, and we moved to Maryland. My parents were true pioneers in every sense of the word. They believed in equal rights for all, wanted to have friends of different ethnicities and wanted to live their lives as an example for truly embracing our humanity. We moved to a new, modern city called Columbia, Maryland in 1969—which is the foundation for the story which you are about to read.

I went away to college in 1978, in Hartford, Connecticut, where I met my husband. He was a handsome, bright, intellectual guy who definitely thought outside the box. He was from central New Hampshire and was the son of a Congregationalist minister and a 4th grade teacher. His mom came from a very small town in the Sunapee mountains, where she went to school in a one room school house. Quite a difference from the numbered schools of my mom's elementary education in the Bronx and my dad's schooling in the primarily Jewish neighborhood on Long Beach Long Island, New York. His Dad came from a tiny town called Hill, which was one of the first "planned" communities. The original town of Hill was flooded when a Dam broke, and the entire town was moved to a different location. Our wedding was a menagerie of people from all backgrounds and beliefs — a party that everyone in attendance will always remember. And so began another phase of my multi-dimensional life.

Now, back to my purpose... When I moved to Florida (for the second time) in 2013, I was dropped (kind of like the stork dropping the baby into the waiting arms of its mother in the movie Dumbo) into an established spiritual community. In the first several months, I attended several psychic fairs and had a few readings. In each reading there was a recurring theme: I came to Florida to find my purpose. One woman said I was going to make something with my hands. I'm really not crafty, so I couldn't imagine what that could be. One said I was going to teach spirituality, maybe yoga. I'm open to spiritual practice — I had been raised with an open mind and even learned transcendental meditation as a child when my mother took me to a yogi — but I am far from a "spirit-head." Teaching it didn't really spark any interest either. In my third reading, I was told that I was going to write a book and it would teach many people about love, peace, and what it meant to be open-minded. FLASH — the light bulb went off above my head.

I was going to write a book about growing up in Columbia and how that unique experience influenced me, my family, my life, and as you will see, the lives of hundreds of thousands of people. It is a story of love, peace, understanding, compassion and a true embracing of the differences between people. It's about the acknowledgment that we are really all part of one race... the HUMAN race.

NINETEEN- to 23-passenger Minibus is designed for extended stop-and-start driving. System is expected to eliminate need of second car for many families, and will bring much of Columbia within easy reach of every resident.

Exhibit center interior. For many, this was their first Columbia experience. Thousands flocked to the Frank Gehry–designed building to discover Columbia's hopes and dreams; some decided to make it their home. *Robert Tennenbaum.*

CHAPTER 1:

Columbia Maryland—a New Kind of City

Columbia, Maryland is the brainchild of builder and developer James Rouse. (Rouse was also renowned for designing mega malls like New Jerseys' Paramus Park and Echelon Malls, The Mall of America and The Mall in Columbia.) He had a dream to create a community where people from all backgrounds, religions, colors, socio-economic standing, or any other form of diversity could live side-by-side, in peace and harmony—a "New Utopia" he liked to call it. During a time of social unrest in the early and mid-1960's, the concept of people all living together in peace was extremely appealing to Rouse. Not only could people searching for a more diverse and peaceful way to live find a home, Rouse could show the world that all types of people COULD live together in peace. I've always referred to it as "The Grand Social Experiment"—one that Rouse planned to conduct on a very large scale.

So what makes Columbia so different? Why did Columbia have this special draw for people with open minds and hearts? To truly illustrate an answer to this question, you have to go back to the mid-1960's—the time when the seed of an idea called "Columbia" was planted.

Columbia is a planned community that opened in 1967 in Howard County, Maryland—the second wealthiest county in the United States, according to 2013 U.S. Census Bureau figures. Creator and developer James Rouse saw the new community in terms of human values, rather than merely economics and engineering. Columbia was intended to both eliminate the inconveniences of current subdivision designs of the time, as well as to eliminate racial, religious, and class segregation within the city. Columbia has consistently ranked in the top ten of CNN Money's Best Places to Live in America.

Rouse purchased a very large tract of farm land that was located in central Howard County, on both sides of the county's only main road, Route 29. All of this land was to become the home for the 100,000+ residents that call Columbia home today. Only this was 1964 and ground had not been broken.

The Town Center, constructed in 1967, was designed to be the business and social center for all Columbians to share. The central feature of Town Center is Lake Kittamaqundi . Its name, taken from the first recorded Native American settlement in Howard County, means "meeting place." The lake is a 27-acre man-made reservoir complete with a boardwalk and fishing docks. There was a pier with a bell tower, a public dock with paddle boats and canoes to rent (and recently added Swan Boats) and a walking path that goes all the way around the lake. In the center of the common area is the famous People Tree sculpture, by Pierre du Fayet, which was dedicated on June 21, 1967. It is a golden, dandelion-like structure that towers about 30 feet in the air. The branches of the tree are made in the likeness of many people, reaching up.

On the banks of the lake sit the American City Building, an 11-story office building (now connected to The Mall by a pedestrian overpass), the Columbia Association Building, a 4-story office building overlooking the lake, the Exhibit Center and the Rouse Building. The Rouse Building, a much loved landmark in Columbia because of its modern and terraced architecture that graced the terraced lakefront park, was home to offices and a beautiful function room with decking right along the lakeshore. (The Rouse Building now houses a Whole Foods.) On the lakefront ground level of the Columbia Association Building is Clyde's, a restaurant, which was, and remains, a favorite meeting place for the new town.

A large fountain welcomed Kittamaqundi guests to the lakefront, with its waterfalls coming down like curtains into a circular pool. The design allowed visitors to walk underneath and behind the falls. A bronze statue of Rouse and his brother Willard (by artist William F. Duffy) was later added on the tiered plaza that leads down to the water's edge.

I often say that I am "a Product of Columbia." I was raised in Columbia and lived there from its infancy, watching it grow, while I grew. I clearly remember our first trip to Columbia; seeing this "space age" city, visiting the lake, walking under the fountain and feeding the ducks on the boardwalks by the boathouse. My family moved to Columbia in August of 1969. I was about to enter 4th grade and my brother was going into 2nd. My parents purchased their first home, a three-story end unit townhouse, for $29,000. We were one of the first 500 families in Columbia. The early Columbians refer to themselves as "Pioneers." (See Pioneers in Chapter 2.)

The lakefront amphitheater was a place for Columbians and other visitors to gather on warm summer evenings to listen to live music, watch a family movie, or just come with a picnic and sit on the beautifully manicured, terraced lawn that leads to the waterfront. There was such a shared passion for the city. Rouse shared his passion openly and that passion was contagious. The Exhibit Center building housed a scale model of his vision and information about Columbia, including its neighborhoods and plans for the future. It had a true 60's/70's style viewing room that had a three-screen slide-show with changing pictures of smiling faces of families of every shape and color, along with some of Columbia's most beautiful statuary and green areas. A low voice spoke about the idea of Columbia and of all that the planned community could offer. My brother and I appeared in one of the slides a few months after we had moved in. What a surprise that was, seeing our faces up on the big screen! The room was very "period" with brown, gold, burnt orange and olive green carpeted walls and carpeted blocks for seats in the center.

I can remember seeing all the happy young families walking the grounds of Town Center. Seeing all the families and children enjoying the lakefront together made me feel proud that my parents wanted us to live there. I can still see the dirt cul-de-sac with the half built homes and the construction equipment noisily breaking ground at the top of the street.

Our home was in the first row completed on our street. By the time we were ready to move in, there were two completed rows and several others were near completion. It was so exciting getting ready to move into our own home and I could tell how proud my parents were. By the time half of our street was complete, the big tar trucks came in to lay the road. It was a very hot day in early August. We came the next day and had to park at the top of the hill, in the school parking lot. By evening the tar had cooled and we were able to bring the cars down. I could still smell the greasy, rubber-like smell of the new tar. That weekend it was even hotter than it had been when they laid the street. We were heading up to the playground at the elementary school, which was adjacent to our street. My flip flops felt sticky in the new macadam. I wondered why the cars didn't get stuck. I was excited — the next weekend we were moving to Columbia!

In the beginning, we would go down to Lake Kittamaqundi almost every weekend. We loved to go to the exhibit center to bask in the glory of our new community. We would bring our guests who were visiting our new home to the exhibit center so they could see and understand the wonderful place we had come to live. There was a pop-art map of Columbia available at the exhibit center. I think every kid I knew had one of those maps on the wall in their bedroom. It was so exciting to be a part of this big social experiment called "Columbia," and the map was so colorful and fun.

Rouse's Columbia was made up of ten villages, each made up of three or four neighborhoods. Each village had a shopping center

with a "Village Center" that had a place for meetings, a little theater, community offices and studios. There were little mom-and-pop
shops as well as a grocery store and a few offices. The first two villages also had the middle school and high school and an "Interfaith
Center." Neighborhoods within the villages shared a community
center, an elementary school, a convenience store and a pool.

The Interfaith Center was an integral part of the grand design.
The center had a few different "sanctuary" rooms, several classrooms, a common area and offices. The building itself did not have
any religious symbols in its architecture or interior design. Synagogues and churches of different denominations rented space in the
Interfaith Center and practiced their faith under one roof. Religious
art, artifacts and symbols were allowed only during services and cer-
emonies and had to be portable. It was not uncommon for different
congregations to come together to celebrate common holidays and
their diversity. For those of us who grew up in Columbia, this was
the norm. Although we all knew that Columbia did things differently, we didn't know any other way, and living in this environment
seemed totally normal.

At first, there was only the Village of Wilde Lake, which was

Opening day celebration for the Wilde Lake Interfaith Center on August 3, 1970. (Photo Don Reichle)

named after Frazer Wilde, past chairman of Connecticut General Life Insurance. The Wilde Lake Village Center had a "Giant" grocery store (which was torn down in 2013, which was quite a blow to many of the "Pioneers" of Columbia) a drug store, a butcher shop (called The Butcher Shop), a cheese shop (called The Cheese Shop), a shoe repair store, a dry cleaner, a Chinese restaurant (called The Tiki Room) and some offices. There was also a plaza area in the middle of the shopping center with a children's play area, and in the center of the 2-acre plaza stood a sculpture which is a three figure representation of family love. It was also designed by Pierre du Fayet.

The first neighborhoods were Faulkner Ridge (named after poet/writer William Faulkner), Bryant Woods (named after poet William Cullen Bryant) and Running Brook (named for a work of poet Robert Frost). Many other street names in the neighborhoods were taken from titles and phrases from the poet's works. I grew up on Tolling Clock Way in the neighborhood Faulkner Ridge in the Village of Wilde Lake.

Today, Columbia is the second largest city in Maryland, second to Baltimore (as of the 2010 census) and is now home to nearly 100,000 people. It is a beautifully laid out suburban mecca that flanks US Route 29. From the highway you can see the downtown area lake, lined by modern (if 1960's is still considered modern) office build-ngs, lighted pathways and terraced common areas. At night, the downtown area shines like a gem along the Howard County roadside. Columbia is home to a big and very popular mall, surrounded by many restaurants, a large movie theater with I-Max, beautiful new condominium apartments and modest, not-too-tall office buildings. Columbia has very strict building ordinances, and buildings cannot be taller than 12 stories. An 8,000 seat concert venue, the Meriweather Post Pavilion, and the adjoining park, Symphony Woods, are also right off of Route 29. Many businesses make Columbia their home base, but more than anything, Columbia is all about its residents. It is truly a bedroom community. A great place for commuters, located almost exactly at the halfway point between Baltimore and Washington D.C.

Today, like any big city, Columbia has its share of problems. Home break-ins, robberies, and although very rare, even murders. But Columbia is different. People who choose to make Columbia their home choose the community for its diversity, its shared religious spaces, its reserved open space land, bike paths, and small neighborhood feeling. When you ask almost anyone who lives in Columbia why they choose to live in Columbia, the answer usually includes, "It's a great place to raise kids."

James Rouse, left, and Frazar Wilde flank the plaque that was installed for the dedication of Wilde Lake. During the ceremony, Rouse praised Wilde, calling him "one special, indispensable hero," for responding to an "outrageous proposal" and partnering in the Columbia project by providing the necessary financing.

CHAPTER 2:

The Pioneers

As noted in Chapter 1, the first residents of Columbia referred to themselves as "The Pioneers." The reference to The Pioneers was originally used for the first 100 families, but over time has encompassed the first 500 families. This new city was built on a promise of a world where all people from a variety of backgrounds could live together—THRIVE together! Most people who came to Columbia in those early years came because of what Columbia represented. Yes, it was a new and modern city, with peaceful open space areas, modern amenities, new homes and could be a pleasant place for any family to live. But Columbia spoke to people at a very different level.

My parents, as an example, wanted to buy their first home in Columbia so they could raise their children in an environment where their faith (Judaism) would be honored, not ridiculed; where we could meet children who were different than ourselves, without having to deal with stigma and prejudice. My mom and dad, although not hippies by any stretch of the imagination, did embrace many of the ideals of the sixties counter-culture: peace, love, understanding, racial equality, women's liberation, etc.

As I mentioned previously, when I was only a baby, my parents moved to Newport News, Virginia so my dad could work on a naval submarine. (He was an electrical engineer.) My dad was at work and my mom had taken me outside to play. Once we were outside for a few minutes, my mom had noticed that the other moms in the neighborhood had taken their children back inside. That night, neighborhood men burned a cross on our front yard. We moved out of Newport News that next weekend. From that point on, as my parents had told me, they wanted to take a stand against prejudice and social injustice. As you will read, they did just that.

For my mom, her desire to embrace the diverse world we live in, and to live as an example to others, started at an early age. When my mom was a pre-teen, during a time when her parents were divorcing, she stayed with an uncle in Oklahoma over the summer. Her uncle was a country doctor. In the late 1940's, prejudice, segregation and bigotry were the norm—but not for my mom's uncle. He believed in the worth and dignity of all people and that everyone should have access to medical care. My mom told the story of how she used to go with her uncle on house calls, visiting the entirely black, poverty-stricken rural areas several miles from where he lived. She would sit in his big car (usually in the rumble seat) and wait for him while he treated someone in the house.

Often he would return to the car with a big sack of potatoes or other food or items in exchange for his services. Her uncle nearly lost his license to practice medicine because he routinely made it a practice to treat the "black folk". His determination to treat the medical needs of all people, without regard to race, even in the face of being ostracized by the medical community, inspired my mother. From that summer on, my mom was on a mission.

My mother and father were high school sweethearts. My mom, her mom and her siblings moved from their apartment in the Bronx to Long Beach, Long Island, living in a modest home. My grandmother was an air-raid warden in the post-WWII years. My dad, who lived in Long Island, came from an upper middle-class family. They were pretty conservative. So, when my dad met this outspoken, artist/social activist, they were concerned… but the rest was history. They married when my father finished college. He studied engineering and my mom studied art education. He then served two years in the Coast Guard, sailing aboard The Eagle. I was born in September 1960, and my brother was born in 1962.

My dad marched on Washington when Dr. Martin Luther King, Jr. gave the remarkable "I Have a Dream" speech. I was only just turning 3 years old in August of 1963 and didn't really understand what was going on. I do remember my mom seeming nervous about where dad was that day. She stayed glued to the radio and was listening to news stories. It was not until I was in middle school that I really understood what my dad had done. A young, white, Jewish boy (only 27 at the time) marched on Washington for civil rights and was witness to one of the most (if not the most) poignant speeches and impactful days for social justice of all times.

I remember heated conversations my parents had with my grandparents (on my father's side) about the social unrest they saw and heard on the news. I don't remember specifics, but I certainly remember the tone of the conversation and understood that my parents were not in agreement with my grandparents and were quite passionate about their position. In retrospect, I don't think my grandparents were thrilled with the idea of Columbia and would have preferred my parents move into a nice Jewish neighborhood, preferably back on Long Island. That was not going to happen. So, against voiced opposition, my parents made the move to Columbia and the rest was history — my history.

It wasn't more than a couple of days after we moved into our townhouse that we started meeting other people in our neighborhood: young families and couples of all different ethnicities, colors, religions. I remember my first day of school, only a few weeks after we moved in, and noticing all of the different kinds of kids in my class. In my mind, I thought this was interesting and exciting. In my previous school, I had one Black and one Asian classmate and they weren't treated very nicely by the other kids, or the teacher for that matter. In this new school, the teachers were younger and all of the kids played together without fighting. I felt pretty special, getting to live in Columbia. And our schools were special, too.

Another feature of the Columbia "social experiment" was that schools were not to have any classroom walls. All Columbia schools were "Open Space Schools."

Open Space Schools were a new concept in learning. The idea being that by taking down the physical walls of the classrooms, the students were more open to learning and the teachers could be more open about teaching. I remember walking into "Team 4" and there were four different class areas. Each class area was divided by a few little portable walls that were about as tall as I was. The walls would get moved around with the Team so there could be larger spaces for combined classes and smaller spaces when there was smaller, more focused learning going on. The material that had to be covered over the school year was broken out into segments and students would work at their own pace. Those who were quick studies and worked well independently could finish work sooner and get additional projects for extra credit and those who were slower learners had more time with the teacher, so they could really understand the learning materials. There were both teacher's assistants and parent helpers for each Team. Teams were broken out in two grade level learning groups. These Teams (which did have a wall separating them) were in four separate sections of the school building, with the Media Center (library) in the center of the school. Each Team room was open to the Media Center. One of the 4th/5th grade teachers was a bee keeper. In the middle of the Media Center there was a big, papier-mâché tree, with birds and other forest animals in its branches and in the center of the tree, was a bee hive.

COLUMBIA'S SECOND SCHOOL: This is how the Faulkner Ridge Elementary School in The Village of Wilde Lake will look when completed. Architects McLeod, Ferrara & Ensign A.I.A. of Washington are the designers.

Another feature of Columbia's education system was that all the primary schools were within walking distance. During my years growing up in Columbia, I never took a bus to school. The elementary schools were in each neighborhood, so the younger children never had more than a 5-minute walk to school. There were a small number of outlying homes, so there was a bus or two, but for the most part, kids walked to school. My school was adjacent to my street so I

was there in a manner of a few minutes. And, get this…kids walked to school without their parents taking them. It was safe! We walked or rode our bikes, and there were plenty of bike racks to lock up our bikes. There was a big crew of 4th and 5th grade Safety Patrols that would help the younger kids cross the streets as they walked to school. The middle school and high school were near the village centers. The neighborhoods that comprised the first two villages all went to the same middle and high school. My walk to middle school took 10 to 15 minutes. There were many more busses at the middle and high school, as some of the kids had to come from further away than a mile.

Columbia also had public transportation. In the original plans, Rouse had envisioned a monorail moving between all of the village centers. Although a monorail never materialized, there was the Columbus. The Columbus traveled around town: each bus line had a different color and the buses colors matched their line. In the beginning, you could only ride the bus with a bus pass that you would purchase at your village center. In time, the buses took coins as well. It was an efficient and easy-to-use system, especially in the beginning, when there was only the Village of Wilde Lake, and then the second Village of Harpers Choice. As Columbia grew, the Columbus became a less attractive option, but is still being used today. Getting around Columbia by person power was also well thought out. Almost all main roads had bike lanes and wide sidewalks. Connecting each neighborhood and village was a web of bike/walking paths through beautiful forested areas, preserved in Columbia's plans that included over 3500 acres of park lands.

Part of Rouse's vision was that Columbians could easily immerse themselves in the beauty of nature.

The open space includes 268 footbridges, 170 tot-lots, the 40-acre Symphony Woods, 40 ponds and lakes, and natural open space areas interlaced by more than 93.5 miles of pathways for walking, biking and jogging. The 3 main lakes include Town Center's Lake Kittamaqundi, Wilde Lake (built while the first village was taking shape) and Lake Elkhorn. Together with plazas, picnic areas, public areas, tennis courts and two parcourse fitness trails, Columbia's open space is a feature that draws many outdoor enthusiasts to Columbia as an alternative to standard suburban and urban lifestyles. The Columbia Association Open Space Management team plans, develops, manages and maintains Columbia's impressive green spaces. In addition, each village has an Open Space Committee, made up of community

Informal Construction crew at work on dam in one of the streams of the Village of Wilde Lake. Woods and streams are but a short walk from every neighborhood in Columbia.

volunteers who assist the Columbia Association (CA) in managing the appearance of the village's open spaces.

The Columbia Association (CA), which utilizes one of the original buildings in the town center lakefront area, maintains all that is Columbia, from the open spaces, to roads, building ordinances, business licensing, the pools, neighborhood and village centers amongst many other things. Residents who own property in Columbia pay CA fees each year — a type of HOA fee of sorts, but much more specific and involved. When you own in Columbia, you take part in "The Covenant" which is a very strict set of rules that all residents must follow. The primary goal of the covenant is to ensure the beauty and integrity of Columbia is maintained by all of its residents. There are rules regarding what color you can paint your house, where things can be built, what you can plant, and how late you can party outside and how loud you can be. Want to build a fence around your yard? You've got to get permission from CA, and the fence must meet all covenant requirements. Want to paint your house blue? You better move to Laurel. You're a business and you want to put a big neon sign in front of your establishment? Don't count on it. There are to be no "eye sores" in Columbia, no sky scrapers and no overgrown yards.

All in all, the CA fees are reasonable and the covenant works to protect Columbia residents and the beauty of this city. If you want to use all of the facilities like the fitness centers and pools, that is another fee. Sliding scale is available for residents with low and modest incomes and for families that can afford it; the prices are really no different than belonging to a swim club. My parents were not "well off" but managed to maintain a CA Pass for our family.

Columbia had all the suburban perks: Swimming pools, playgrounds, scouts, community sports teams, nature camps, and we participated in everything. Throughout my childhood, I honestly do not remember there ever being fights or negative behaviors of any racially motivated nature between the kids. Everyone mixed together and got along. We had block parties and everyone came out and socialized. We had holiday parties in the village center and at the Interfaith Center, where we all shared stories about how our families celebrated the holidays. We learned about Easter and Passover, Christmas and Hanukkah, Buddha and Krishna.

When we first arrived in Columbia, my family had yet to affiliate with any synagogue that was practicing at the Interfaith Center. When I was very small, I don't recall having ever gone to synagogue except for a wedding or a Bar or Bat Mitzvah. My parents didn't "fit in" to the more traditional form of religious practice. So, along with about a dozen other families who felt much the same way, a new kind of Judaism was born in Columbia.

Our little congregation, that met at "The Slayton House" in the Wilde Lake Village Center building, called themselves "Innovative Jews." To begin with, we were a congregation without a Rabbi. We came together on Friday nights or Saturday mornings and people shared readings, stories, and verses from the Old Testament. We sang songs with guitars as accompaniment and there was dancing and tambourine playing. It was great! After a few months, the group received a letter from a Rabbi who had heard about this little lay-lead congregation in this new city called Columbia, and he thought his beliefs and methods would fit this little group. This Rabbi was not traditional and he didn't really fit-in with other more structured and conservative congregations. Even more reformed synagogues were too conservative for this Rabbi. Along with the letter, the Rabbi sent a copy of his books, "AMEN - The Diary of Rabbi Martin Siegel" and the rest was history. My history.

My parents not only believed in the concept of a culturally-rich and diverse place to raise a family but wanted to reflect that passion in their own family. In 1971 my family decided to adopt a child. My parents explained that we were going to welcome a baby who was considered "hard to place," meaning a child of mixed heritage. Late in 1971 we welcomed Matt to our family — a "mixed race" child with Black, White and Native American heritage. He was five months old.

In 1973, another sibling was adopted, Rachel, 10 months old, also of mixed heritage. At that time, having a multi-racial family and adopting children of a different heritage than your own was very unusual. Had we lived in a different community, I anticipate our experience would have been much different. Living in Columbia, this rainbow family (my mom liked to call us that) was welcomed with open arms and no judgement. My siblings grew up in a loving home and loving community, where their ethnicity and family circumstances were appreciated and embraced. My parents were always trendsetters. Over the years, other friends of the family moved to Columbia and families we knew also adopted "hard to place" children.

CHAPTER 3:

Testimonials from Pioneers

"The ultimate purpose [of planning and architectural design], it seems to me, must be the improvement of mankind."

~James Rouse

Photo courtesy of The Columbia Archives

"We created ways for people to care more deeply about one another, to stimulate, encourage, release creativity, minimize intolerance and bigotry."

~James Rouse

THE ROUSE COMPANY | INTRA–OFFICE MEMORANDUM

August 22, 1967

TO: Developers and their Sales Associates at Columbia

FROM: James W. Rouse

. .   .   .

RE: Equality of Opportunity in Housing Policy

It is important for all of us who are selling houses or lots or renting apartment in Columbia to understand that Columbia is a truly open city.

Simply stated, we are "color-blind." This means that every person or family coming to Columbia to seek a lot, an apartment, a house; to start a business; to play golf, tennis, ride horseback, sail, swim, or use any other facility open to the public will be treated alike regardless of whether the color of his skin is white, black, brown, or yellow. All people will be shown the courtesy and attention by sales personnel that is appropriate to their interest regardless of color. They will be free to select any lot, house, or apartment without restriction, persuasion, or influence because of their race.

No agreements or understanding will be extended to any person or family that he will be "protected" against having a neighbor of a race different from his own.

We really mean that Columbia is an open city. We are convinced that if this is clear to everyone--if all doors are really open--if there is no place for anyone to hide, then no one need be afraid; need seek protection; need knock down any closed doors. It is our hope that Columbia's policy as to race may be so clear and vivid from the beginning that it will be unmistakable to everyone.

If you have any questions about any of this, give me a call in order that we can talk it over. We ask that you make it a fixed policy in your company for a copy of this memorandum to be provided every person who deals with the public in any way in order that there can be no room for misunderstanding among us.

James W. Rouse

JWR/ehk

Letter courtesy of The Columbia Archives

An Intra-Office Memorandum from James W. Rouse, August 22, 1967.

Re: Equality of Opportunity in Housing Policy

It is important for all of us who are selling houses or lots or renting apartments in Columbia to understand that Columbia is a truly open city.

Simply stated, we are "color-blind." This means that every person or family coming to Columbia to seek a lot, an apartment, a house; to start a business; to play golf, tennis, ride horseback, sail, swim, or use any other facility open to the public, will be treated alike regardless of whether the color of his skin is white, black, brown, or yellow. All people will be shown the courtesy and attention by sales personnel that is appropriate to their interest, regardless of color. They will be free to select any lot, house, or apartment without restriction, percussion, or influence because of their race.

No agreements or understanding will be extended to any person or family that he will be "protected" against having a neighbor of a race different from his own.

We really mean that Columbia is an open city. We are convinced that if this is clear to everyone – if all doors are really open and there is no place for anyone to hide – then no one need be afraid; need seek protection; need knock down any closed doors. It is our hope that Columbia's policy as to race may be so clear and vivid from the beginning that it will be unmistakable to everyone.

If you have any questions about any of this, give me a call in order that we can talk it over. We ask that you make it a fixed policy in your company for a copy of this memorandum to be provided every person who deals with the public in any way in order that there can be no room for misunderstanding among us.

Signed James W. Rouse

In the following pages you will read testimonials from some of the earliest residents of Columbia. Some will be from the Pioneers themselves, while others from their children or future generations.

Columbia Pioneers

Ken Carlson

Ken Carlson was part of the original partnerships of Rouse and the first builder, James Ryland of Ryland Homes.

"In 1964 my family and I were proceeding from New York City to Alabama and on the way we stopped in colorful Howard County for lunch. I picked up a newspaper and low and behold, one of the headlines read it was rumored that someone had put together a large tract of land in the sum of about 15,000 acres for a housing development.

While I was working in the housing business in Alabama, I went up to Pittsburgh to meet with James Ryland. I had been studying the current housing market and when I was talking with Jim I told him that the Baltimore-Washington area was one of the few untapped markets for a standing housing program. That conversation led to Jim Ryland and I meeting with Jim Rouse, in early 1966, to discuss the potential of doing a housing development in the new city of Columbia, Maryland. The result of this conversation was a 1,500 developed lot option program where Rouse would develop the lots and Ryland would build.

In 1967, Ryland Homes had constructed six model homes for the Columbia City opening. At the time of the opening, Ryland already had 28 signed contracts. This was unusual, as the gates were locked and there were no roads paved in the city. So these 28 people who signed contracts had been taken in around locked gates and over dirt roads and still wanted to sign contracts for new homes. The roads into the model homes were actually paved at night, right before the grand opening of the new city.

Over the next 12 years Ryland built over 3,000 houses in Columbia. More than all the other builders combined. I was the General Manager for the Columbia project for Ryland Homes. Interestingly, we were the first family to purchase a residential lot and build a home in Columbia. The house was located at the corner of Waterfowl Terrace and Green Mountain Circle. The house we built there had "Cedar Shakes," (a more rustic, non-uniform, wooden shingle) which became a symbol for the Ryland Homes business in Columbia.

What impressed me and my family about Columbia was the potential for quality family living. Schools and parks were located in each of the neighborhoods and were in dead-end cul-de-sacs, thereby permitting children to attend school and enjoy the playgrounds without having to cross any of the major roads or thoroughfares. The sense of community was a major consideration for the original residents of Columbia. The approximately 100 original residents that are called "The Pioneers" have, over the years, come together for various events and reunions."

Chaya Kaplan

Chaya Kaplan is a contented woman, wife of 55 years, mother of 3, grandmother of 8, born and bred New Yorker, active participant in the Howard County Jewish Community, and Co-Founder of A-OK Mentoring-Tutoring, Inc. and the Youth Development Coalition.

"My husband and I and our three preschool children moved to Columbia in September 1969. We chose Columbia for what it represented: An experiment in building a successful, diverse community where families, individuals, and people of all ages, races, ethnicities, and faiths could live and grow together. On our street of 15 houses, with diverse individuals and families, we all were good neighbors, some of us becoming lifelong friends.

Four years later my family moved to a larger house in a different neighborhood in Columbia. We found ourselves with two wonderful next-door neighbors—on one side an African American family with three teenage children, and on the other a couple, the wife from Ecuador and the husband, an American, who grew up on a farm in the Mid-West. We have been friends and neighbors with these families for 40+ years.

Although we developed ties to a varied group of people in our immediate neighborhoods, our deepest friendships generally developed through our participation in the organized Jewish community, especially the Columbia Jewish Congregation — people most like us. Interesting!

On a final note, as a retired social worker I became interested in doing something about the cadre of children in Howard County who were not succeeding in our nationally ranked public school system, who were largely minority children from low income families. In 2003, I helped develop a mentoring-tutoring program to address the needs of these children. In school year 2013-14, A-OK Mentoring-Tutoring, Inc. had 95 adult volunteers serving approximately 240 children. A-OK is an immensely rewarding volunteer endeavor for me, as I read teacher accounts of improvements in their students.

I am grateful for the choice my family made in 1969 to live in Columbia, a place I have always felt at home, and thank Jim Rouse for his faith and inspiring vision."

Sue Hallman

"I first moved to Columbia in 1972, shortly after I started working for The Rouse Company. I didn't really know much about Columbia at the time, but I am a quick learner.

Jim Rouse was such a visionary. His dream was of a city where everyone was welcome and could find a home. Over the years, I've seen much change with the company that built the City of Columbia. Things changed most when Mr. Rouse retired from The Rouse Company in 1984 and moved on to The Enterprise Foundation.

Mike Spears took over the role of CEO at The Rouse Company. He was so like Mr. Rouse and the company would have continued in the same light had he lived. Mike Spears passed away in a tragic accident in August of 2000. Following Mr. Spear's death, the leadership of the company clearly took a different path and now the company is gone and in August of 2014, their beautiful Headquarters Building on Lake Kiddamaqundi is now a Whole Foods store.

My first Columbia home was in the apartment complex which, at the time, was called Tor and was situated on the highest part of the city with the back side overlooking Route 29. The best part of living at Tor was that you could sit on Tor Hill and have a great view of the annual 4th of July fireworks. Of course, in 1972, the fireworks didn't draw the crowd that it does today."

Claudia Wehdeking Friend

"We wanted to make a fresh start when we saw the Columbia Exhibit in the pavilion in 1968. Joe was a CDR in the Navy. We had moved several times and always had to buy a house because rentals were unavailable. We liked the plan James Rouse proposed for open housing and cultural and ethnic diversity. We liked the idea of village centers and that our four kids could walk to Faulkner Ridge Elementary School, Wilde Lake Middle and High Schools. This plan allowed me to work full time because I did not have to drive our kids around for after school activities. We and our kids enjoyed meeting so many wonderful, new people and made many friends. I wanted a recreational community with swimming pools, bike paths and playgrounds for our kids. We are still grateful to live here!"

Children of the Pioneers

"I arrived in Columbia the summer of 1968. We lived in the Concord House until our house was built in Hobbit›s Glen. I attended Bryant Woods Elementary for 3rd, Faulkner Ridge 4th and 5th, Wilde Lake Middle for 6th and 7th then Harpers Farm Middle School for 8th and WLHS for 9th through 12th, so witnessed Columbia as it developed from many perspectives. I concur with many comments about lack of "race" in Columbia. My best friends were black; some were Jewish as well as white. Exposure to different cultures, food and religions enriched my childhood. I was not exposed to racism until I left Columbia for college; luckily it was minor. Unfortunately, some of my black friends saw racism at its ugliest level. We lived in a utopia, protected in many respects from harsh environments. One might think that we were too sheltered; however, I believe we were strong of convictions, accepting of change and differences and better citizens because of it."

"I was a 1967 'Child of Columbia.' I didn't know racism. Blacks dated whites. Planned community, walking paths, and a safe, good community. My home. Columbia was such a positive and proud experience for me, growing up."

"I was born in Columbia in 1972. There was no such thing as race to me growing up. The first time it ever became an issue for me was when I was visiting family in the mid-west when I was about 12, and my cousin told me we were going to hang out with her 'black friend.' I was dumbfounded and could not comprehend why she would call her friend that, instead of just by her name. As I got older, I became more aware of the little bubble I lived in growing up in Columbia, with most of the outer world seeming more prejudiced. I became very proud to live in that bubble, and to this day am proud, and grateful, to have grown up in it."

"Columbia Association (CA) was hiring teens to do jobs in the community. One I was involved with was planting the trees between Faulkner Ridge and Bryant Woods... Lived in the fourth house built in Columbia, a Ryland model on Evening Wind Ct..."

"I was 5 when we moved there from Rockville. We moved to a new house on Our Time Lane. I started Kindergarten at Stevens Forest Elementary in 1972...memories of walking to school on the paths and riding my bike to school were such great experiences, going to the indoor and outdoor pools all over Columbia, my dad dropping me and my friends off at Columbia Mall and buying albums and 45's, going to the arcade, going to the movie theater, my dad and I getting a paddle boat on the lake, my brother and I walking across the lake from Tor Apts. to the mall, going to Symphony Woods and the petting zoo. The first concerts I seen at Merriweather Post Pavilion were Captain and Tennille, Sha Na Na and Kenny Loggins. My sister drove a Colum-bus and would take me with her on her routes; I met so many great people! I could go on and on!"

"We moved to Columbia when I was 3, left when I was 15. When I went to college in Boston in the eighties I was completely in the closet about racism. This led to an interesting first few years in that great city. I went to all the places that I wasn›t supposed to be in, just because I did not know any better. This was during a time that Boston was still reeling from busing. I also was often the first African American girl that my Sicilian, Italian, Greek, or Irish boyfriends brought home. I could have been an alien from a strange planet but I know my lack of color awareness taught many around me to look at life the same way."

"I think the saddest day for me was after my mom passed we had to move my dad to Virginia to be with my brother. That meant selling my family's home in Faulkner Ridge. Our family was one of the original families to move into Columbia, just prior to the city's first birthday. My parents were one of the original people to buy a Ryland Home... When we started first grade... we played all over our neighborhood, including down by the creek, at the school, in the street, riding our bikes all over... I'd go to CT to visit my cousin and she would tell me that in the bubble world I lived in, maybe people were different than they were up there, as there was so much prejudice. I didn't know what to do with it. I told her that was not how things were and they were people just like us. She wasn't happy. If I'm in a bubble world, I'll stay here!"

"Columbia is so special, and so successful. James Rouse took everything into account. He made it about people, nature, architecture, innovative concepts, education, recreation, religion, the arts, shopping, everything social in a progressive and responsive fashion. Columbia's exciting and wholesome, about families and individuals who make up the community. The way it was designed for all people, not regardless of, but by inclusion of people of any race, religion or income.

I love the "Village" concept, comprised of neighborhoods. It's organic, and cellular in design with bike paths and woods connecting everything. Plus, there are the lakes! I love how my parents bought one of the very first residential lots (although building the house took longer, being custom) we were within the first 200 families to move here (1967). It was great trick-or-treating when we were in costume because it was the only time when it seemed we didn't know everyone. One time, at Jim Rouse's townhouse, before he moved right down our street, he was exceptionally generous. And, I was impressed when my parents helped found the town's first Jewish congregation. Services took place in family rooms of people's homes. My grandfather's temple provided the Torah, and my father and friends of his built the ark in our basement. But most of all, I love Columbia because it is home."

"My dad worked for the City of Columbia. He did all the grading for all the tot-lots, lakes, pathways and Merriweather Post Pavilion from 1967 to 1988, when he retired. I loved the open spaced school system and Howard County's vo-tech program was a stepping stone for my career." (*Donna Craig*)

"I moved to Partridge Courts in 1970. I moved from Savage, and consider myself a Howard County native and proud Columbian. I remember Columbia as being a welcoming place for newly-divorced moms, like mine. Although many of you remember moving here as full families, my memories are of many newly single mothers at a time that it was unusual. Places like Partridge Courts were a good place for single mothers on smaller incomes." (*Sari Hendrixson Chapman*)

"I'm thinking [I moved to Columbia in] 1972 or 1973. I was in 5th grade at Longfellow Elementary. James Rouse made the rounds to each school. We sat on the floor around him in the Media Center. He talked about his concept of a city with racial diversity, bike paths, the neighborhood/village idea, pools in each neighborhood, and shopping centers in each village. I also remember thinking his plaid pants were interesting." (*Linda (Green) Schreiber*)

"My parents have passed, but I remember what their reasons were for moving to Columbia. They were one of the first [to live] in Wilde Lake. They wanted to be part of Jim Rouse's vision. Mom had read about it in the Sun and thought it would be far better than living in downtown Glen Burnie, MD, which she disliked. Being military we had lived all over the world, and she wanted her retirement home to be perfect. Thus, she was the driving force." (*Gayle Harvey DeBaun*)

"I was turning 7 in 1969 when we moved to Columbia. I remember this statue (right), running through the tunnel, and the fort in Bryant Woods. I thought every town offered what Columbia offered until I moved away when I was in my 30's. I feel lucky to have been a part of the beginning story of Columbia." (*Sue (Sprinsock) Smith*)

A Poem by Bill Lawrence
Columbia

A town never was
that treated all fair
But a man had a notion
To build one there
This place was my backdrop
to learn and to grow
A better setting for youth
I could never know

The scent of May apples
Carried by breeze
Lots filled with tots
And people in trees
Orchards of peaches
To Sewell's we'd go
Fields of strawberries
Walked row by row
And never full baskets in tow!
Meandering paths
With nary a straight line
And the street lamp's glow
My keeper of time

Blankets laid out
like a patchwork quilt
Staking your claim
on the 4th of July
Throwing down quarters
On a Boardwalk tilt
Man, did those summers fly by
My bike was my passport
Gave me freedom to roam
And my folks never worried
Me so far from home
Blue Pools and Half lit Garths
A Camel's back and

Buckleberry
Of course a town like this
finds its roots in poetry
Wide open spaces

Multitudes of faces
You really can't imagine
The number of places
We could go on our own
By foot, bike or board
Miles from home
And our keepers assured
We'd find our way back
Adventures in hand
Scuffed knees and elbows
Life's reprimand
Yet our reward, too
For otherwise there'd be
No proving ground
For courage, conflict and calamity
Hopping fences for a midnight swim
Filling days full of sun to the brim
To those who don't know
This I ask…
Who wouldn't walk
Down a moonlit path?
To my lifelong friends
I humbly bow
Our Columbia youth
A warm blanket now

The Next Generation

Natalie Rivera (my daughter)

Article originally printed in Transformation Magazine.

"While growing up, my holiday home had halls decked with holly, a menorah in the window, and a "Chanamus" tree. I come from a multi-racial, religiously diverse family. My mom's family is Jewish and my dad's family is Christian. I have ancestors who fled the Holocaust, as well as ancestors who came to the United States during the time of the Mayflower.

I am English, Scottish, German, Romanian, Polish, Welch, and Russian. I am a cultural, ethnic, and religious mutt.

My Jewish grandmother once told me a story of going on a house call with her uncle, who was a medical doctor in the 1940's. Unlike most MDs at the time, he felt passionately that everyone, regardless of race or creed, deserved medical care. That day my grandmother accompanied him he made a house call to an African American family, accepting a sack of potatoes as payment for his services. He was ostracized by the medical community for his equal-opportunity healing. His choices impacted my grandmother greatly and, in turn, led her to display decisions in her life that passed a passion for equality and human rights onto my mother, and then onto me.

When my mom was young, my grandparents were active in the Civil Rights Movement. They participated in the March on Washington. They were one of the first families to move into a progressive town called Columbia, MD. My grandparents took their actions one step further, and in the 1970's they adopted two multi-racial children.

How blessed I am to have been exposed to such a powerful example of people who stood up for what they believed in.

Because of my grandparents, I hold myself to a higher standard. I was raised in Columbia until I was six. I lived there long enough for the values of equality, unity, and acceptance to etch deep within my soul. I grew up in a town where my interreligious family was viewed as normal and my interracial extended family was respected and admired. I was "colorblind" and ignorant to the fact that the rest of the world was not like Columbia. I was in for quite a culture shock when my family relocated to New Hampshire, where my dad was raised.

My dad spent part of his childhood living on a farm. While he was growing up, his dad was a Congregationalist Minister and his mother was a teacher. (She even attended school as a child, in a rural, one-room school house.) Interestingly, my understanding of the belief system of the Christian church in which they participated echoes the underlying beliefs of my Jewish background — that a connection to God exists directly within each person. The Congregationalists believe that all people can connect with God directly, and they do not have a hierarchical church structure. My grandparents instilled in me a deep love of nature, the value of family traditions, and the importance of having respect for all people.

Though diverse, my familial influences and beliefs blended peacefully and cohesively. As a result, I developed an unconscious understanding that no person, no deed, no object, and no place stands in between myself and my Creator.

I also became incredibly open minded, accepting, and compassionate, as well as passionate about equality and unity. Unfortunately, my unique perspective has, at times, put me at odds with the rest of the world. As I grew up and was exposed to life beyond the walls of my bubble, I became increasingly idealistic, cynical, and bitter. I could not understand why the rest of the world did not think the way I do.

I remember my first day of second grade, just after I moved to New Hampshire. I came home that afternoon and asked my mom, "Where did all the black kids go?" That year around Christmas, my grade celebrated "Christmas Around the World." We had different stations in which we did crafts and learned about different holidays during the season, such as Kwanza. When we got to the "Israel" station and talked about Chanukah, my life changed.

The teacher told the class that, "Jewish people live in Israel," to which I piped up and said, "No they don't; I live here." The class just stared at me in confusion. Apparently, I was the only Jewish child in my school of 400. The children started asking me questions, the only one I remember being: "Do Jewish people go to Hell?" At the time, I didn't even know what Hell was. From that day forward, I was seen as different.

I attended Christian churches and Sunday school with many of my friends, and I enjoyed most of it. However, one particular incident traumatized me and planted within me a seed of bitterness that it took many years to get over. The Sunday school class was instructed to close our eyes, during which time we were instructed to ask Jesus into our heart. With eyes still closed, the teachers asked us to raise our hands if we had not asked Jesus into our heart. I raised mine, of course—really, really high. (I was always a nonconformist.) I had grown suspect of this character due to observations I'd made interacting with adults at the churches, and I was enthusiastic about standing up against it. What happened next was totally inappropriate, from my adult perspective.

The teachers brought me out into the hall and began berating me. I was overwhelmed, confused, and frightened. I was only 8 years old. I do not remember what they said to me, nor do I think I could have understood it at the time, but I do know that I went home feeling rejected, unworthy, resentful, and with anger in my heart. That day I learned the harsh reality that I did not belong in this world of competition and separatism. These misguided teachers did not succeed at breaking my spirit. Instead, they fueled the fire deep within me that, today, burns and aches to stop suppression, discrimination, and religious holy wars.

Those who found out I was Jewish and responded by stating they would "pray for me" offended me, yes, but they added another log to my fire. I once saw a girl, about 10, walking down the street with her mother, and when they passed a black woman, she asked "Mommy, what happened to that lady's skin?" I was disgusted by her ignorance, but it stoked the embers of my passions.

For years I would not use the word "God" or state that I believed in God, even though I did. If someone asked me if I believed in God, I feared that saying "yes" would imply that I believed in God the way they did, which at the time I felt was a hateful, judgmental, discriminatory God. My parents had attended a Unitarian Universalist church with my sister and myself, and so as an adult I became a member as well. I felt comfortable there, as they were "spiritual" but they did not use the word "God." After years of independent spiritual study I found my way home to the place of tolerance of diversity from which I was raised, and I made peace with the religious beliefs of those who had not yet made peace with me. As an adult, I left the Unitarian church, ironically, because they would not use the word "God."

I have since attended "church" in nature and within the holy temple of my own Being.

Both my little sister and I have selected husbands who are Puerto Rican, keeping with my family's multicultural trend. I have dedicated time to activities that promote diversity awareness and equality, such as running a hip-hop dance group for at-risk, minority students while I was in high school and volunteering for Challenge Day, a diversity awareness and bullying prevention program for middle and high schools. I created a magazine, with the goal in mind of connecting spiritual seekers from every religious, ethnic, and geographic background by focusing on topics that emphasize empowerment, inspiration, and the commonalities within all belief systems.

Only through cooperation and celebration of our diversity can we live and experience the Oneness that we are."

CHAPTER 4:

Open Spaces

The "New City" incorporated two important concepts that garnished the same title: "Open Spaces." During this chapter, I'd like to discuss each of these concepts and their impact on my life in Columbia, as well as my life post-Columbia. It seems to me that Mr. Rouse had the idea that if you took away the boundaries and confines of traditional suburban life—including the actual walls—you could fashion a society that was truly open. For the most part, I think he was spot on.

As mentioned before, part of the plan for Columbia was to set aside land throughout the city that was never to be developed. They called this preserved land, "Open Space." The woods and fields left untouched by development wound their way in and around all of the neighborhoods. Bike paths led you in and out of the woods and connected all of the different neighborhoods. In the earlier days, Columbians could ride their bikes or walk just about anywhere through the web of paths that linked everything together. Along each of these paths you would come upon little ponds, creeks (all the kids loved to play in those creeks) the occasional work-out station and numerous tot-lots or playgrounds. All of the man-made areas along the paths were constructed to blend in with the surroundings. Climbing structures were usually made from dark stained railroad ties and 2x4s. There were often tire swings and rope ladders. Of course, there were chains and poles, but no big red, blue or shiny metal playgrounds. Most consisted of forts, constructed much like Lincoln Logs. I can remember riding my bike and coming across new tot-lots to explore, and walking with my family and our dog along the path and taking a fork in the road that we had yet to explore to see where it would take us. We always found our way into a cul-de-sac or onto a road that we were familiar with and could find our way home.

My brother and I, and all of our friends, would spend hours out in the neighborhood, on the bike paths, playing in the creek, discovering new forts in other tot-lots away from our own block. We were never afraid of strangers lurking in the woods, and parents, in general, were happy to have their kids visit one another through the series of paths that connected our homes. A love for nature and exploration were born from those open spaces. The lakes in Columbia had paths that went all the way around them and open spaces lined their banks. Bike paths would take you to the lakes as well. The Columbia Association sponsored a Summer Camp and it wouldn't surprise me if a majority of the children of the Pioneers went to those day camps. Camp included all of the typical day camp activities, including hiking, boating, fishing, exploring, archery, overnights with campfires and camp songs—all in our own backyards. The open spaces in Columbia made it such a great place to be a kid.

Village Centers also had open spaces. Each village had a center that consisted of a chain grocery store, several mom-and-pop shops, a restaurant or two, a pharmacy, a small liquor shop, a dry cleaner, a barber shop, several office spaces, a community center and a performance hall. In the center there was a large courtyard with fountains, a playground of some type, structures to climb and sit on and grassy or paved areas where people could sit and socialize. There were always tables and chairs set up where neighborhood folks could come to share an ice cream, a coffee, or just sit down and catch up after doing some grocery shopping. The concept of the Village Centers was to keep the small town, main street feel while still providing many of the qualities of a small city.

Each Village had a lake or some type of outdoor element. "Wilde Lake", the first village, had Wilde Lake—a beautiful park with a walking/biking path that went all the way around the lake. There was a damn with a waterfall that offered a beautiful, relaxing place to picnic at its base. There was a catch basin at the bottom of the falls that made a great place for kids to dangle their feet, toss little stones and sometimes even jump in on a hot day. An old stone foundation barn and carriage house were preserved and provided a great backdrop for more picnic areas. The carriage house became the boathouse and there was a floating dock where paddle boats and canoes could be rented. The day camp operated out of the boathouse on Wilde Lake. Townhomes, single family homes and apartment communities lined the shores of Wilde Lake as well. Having a friend live on Wilde Lake was a hot commodity. Everyone wanted to hang out there. Wilde Lake was peaceful and never became a hot spot for loud and destructive parties or a haven for criminals lurking in the bushes, waiting to rob passers-by. It was a safe and wonderful place for kids and adults to visit and everyone did.

Columbia's second village, Harpers Choice, had a Village Center just like Wilde Lake, as well as the meandering bike path connecting all of its neighborhoods. The outdoor feature in Harpers Choice was the Hobbits Glen Golf Club, a beautiful 18-hole golf course, with a community style clubhouse. Hobbits Glen Golf Club was a public club and well loved by golfers in the community and throughout the area. There was a real family feeling to the club and I remember so

"We can't plan effectively for the future growth of American communities unless we start at the beginning and that beginning is people," said Rouse in 1963. A year after Wilde Lake was dedicated, people flock to the shores. The barn is now a part of a place for people.

"We wanted the janitor and the company executive to live in the same neighborhood," Rouse often said. Apartments, townhouses, and single-family houses were built within blocks of each other. In the Bryant Woods neighborhood, Waterfowl Terrace, with its waterfront lots, was set aside for custom-designed homes. Among the residents on that street have been Rouse and his wife Patty, as well Pat Kennedy, who served as president of Columbia Association from 1972 to 1996, and his wife, Ellen. (Photo by Morton Tadder.)

many kids going with their parents to the club and learning to golf. Everyone was welcome there. You didn't have to be rich. There were no restrictions. You didn't have to dress a certain way. You just had to conduct yourself in a civil manner and be welcoming to all those who were there to use the facilities.

Lake Elkhorn was built in Columbia's fourth Village. It was another beautiful lake with a dam and a waterfall that was made of wide cement steps, creating a tiered, slow moving fall that was a favorite place for families to come to cool off on a hot day. Elkhorn had a small tot-lot and a fishing pier, but was built to provide a more county park-like environment, which focused on specific activity locations, rather than the more natural settings found in Wilde Lake. A large gazebo on the far side of the lake was used for birthday parties and special occasions, but it never had the draw that the Town Center and Lake Kittamaqundi did, with its downtown feel and special events, or the hometown feeling of Wilde Lake. There were no homes on the banks, and Lake Elkhorn became a favorite for runners and joggers. Because of its more secluded location, it also became more of a party hangout for the local teens. Even that being the case, during the years my friends and I went to Elkhorn, I never remember there being fights or vandalism. I heard about a few times that cops showed up, but there were never any big busts or problems. Columbia's third lake was just another peaceful place for the residents of Columbia to enjoy.

As Columbia grew, the concept of open spaces continued to be an integral part of the landscape. New bike paths were created to join together each neighborhood and village as the reach of Columbia went deeper into the Howard County farm land.

There were mixed feelings about Columbia's sprawl into Howard County. Longtime residents of Howard County saw Columbia change their landscape from the beautiful, rural farm land of Howard County into a modern and foreign suburban mecca for all different kinds of people from all over the country, and the world. Before Columbia, Howard County, MD was a predominantly white, Southern community that was well established with strong ties to the land. Many families watched as their farm land turned into well-manicured yards, roads and apartment communities. But for a majority of Howard County natives, Columbia did not deter them from continuing to live in the beautiful rolling greens and forested lands of the county they loved. The locals were embraced by the residents of Columbia, and for myself and many of my Pioneer children friends, the remaining farm houses and their families and the older neighborhoods in the area became part of the Columbia experience. Preserving the beauty of the area was also part of the plan.

Open Space Schools

The second "Open Space" concept was that of open space schools. The first open space school in Columbia was Bryant Woods Elementary School. The earliest and youngest residents of Columbia remember starting school at Bryant Woods. The concept of open space learning and team teaching were embodied by their beloved Principal, Mr. V, and Vice Principal, Mr. B. They had a passion for creating a place of learning that embraced each child's individual strengths and rewarded successes, instead of punishing poor performance. This concept of education set the bar for all the teachers and administrators in Bryant Woods Elementary as well as all the other schools to come along in Columbia. The second elementary school built was Faulkner Ridge. The curriculum followed the same structure that was introduced at Bryant Woods.

I started 4th grade at Faulkner Ridge Elementary School. The school fields abutted the street where I lived and it literally took three minutes to walk to school. In third grade, I had been in a traditional elementary school in a temporary school building. It was a one room classroom all day, except for lunch and recess. My new school had no walls. The grades were mixed and a Media Center was the focal point in the center of the building. Around the Media Center were "pods," which consisted of several "home room" classes comprised of two grades within each pod. Students learned in a team teaching environment, within their assigned pod.

Most of our instruction was done with a teacher in the front of the classroom, but part of each class was self-paced work time. Unlike traditional elementary schools, I had a home room and moved to different areas with different teachers for each subject. This approach is typically not used until Junior High/Middle School and High School. The average class was less than 20 students. Each pod had at least one assistant teacher or volunteer as well. There were only a few classes that had walls, including music and art.

The self-paced method of learning was introduced in grade school. Determined by your level of proficiency, you could be in a class with children your own age, a year younger or a year older than yourself. We were able to work at our own level, but also it helped in learning to socialize with kids who were at a different grade level, which provided exposure to different levels of social maturity, making for a more well-rounded and socially capable student. Everyone was accepted by their peers, with no judgment for being "slow" or "a smarty pants." For those children identified as gifted or requiring additional help, accommodations were made for those students as well. Although these students were often taken out of group class time for more individualized learning, it was done in such a fashion that went mostly unnoticed by the rest of the class. When it was time to change classes, if you had individualized learning, you just changed to those classrooms.

Because we all worked at our own pace, when we finished work early, we were given passes to the Media Center where we could read, work on projects or homework or participate in the many learning experiences offered in the Media Center. (I don't remember even having "homework" until middle school.) We were given the benefit of the doubt that we could be responsible for doing our work and that we were going to be where we needed to be, and we met that expectation. This type of learning in the early grades prepared students for an even more open learning environment in the Middle and High Schools.

Wilde Lake Middle School was one of the first of its kind. Not only open space, with team teaching, but the grades were 6-8. In the early 70's, Junior High was grades 7 and 8. Sixth grade was still in the elementary school and 9th graders often remained on the Junior High campus, moving over to the High School in 10th grade. It was the belief of the Columbia school administration that 6th graders were better off learning with children older than themselves. At 11 or 12 years old, a child is more like a pre-teen than a young child. Ninth graders were teenagers and were taking high school classes and belonged with other high school students. I was in the 3rd class to attend Wilde Lake Middle School for all three years. The pods (spoken of earlier in the description of the elementary school) were named after planets. I was in "Jupiter." There were also Mars and Venus pods. The pods had all three grades and for the most part, students remained in the same pod for all three years. The idea was, by working with the same students and teachers for all three years, stronger relationships could be built between the students, creating greater cooperation while learning in a team environment. The teachers got to know the students and were able to determine how best to instruct their smaller pod of students. Each teacher had a specialty and taught one subject, but the teachers worked cooperatively, so the learning and lesson plans related to one another. Students from all three pods attended art, music, theater, gym, sports and school-wide assemblies, together.

Every student was able to find their own path, and the things that they excelled at were identified and supported by the teachers, administrators and other students. I was always the creative type. I loved music and theater. Not only were classes available to grow these passions, but opportunities were provided to truly express my creativity. There were always student performances, art shows, creative writing exhibitions, and the typical student plays and concerts. I wrote a play that was performed for my pod, called "Teachers in Trouble." It had to do with students being given the freedom to express themselves and they ended up taking over the classes from the teachers. I also wrote some political satire songs, which were performed by a handful of my friends in the cafeteria during lunch. "Nixon's screwing up the nation, all the live long day..." I have a feeling this type of performance would not have been allowed anywhere other than Columbia.

The layout of the middle school was much like the elementary school. Pods were separated by walls, but there were no walls within the classroom clusters. Children moved from teacher to teacher within their own pod in a rotation, so there was little need for a schedule or assigned classroom numbers. The art, music, shop and home economics rooms, administrative offices and gymnasium were located around the outer edges of the building and the Media Center was located in the center of the building, accessible from the three pods and the cafeteria. Movement between classes flowed easily and quietly as I recall. I don't remember a mad dash to get from one class to another. Lockers were spread out throughout the center of the school. Students could freely use the Media Center. Books and audio visual equipment were easily accessible and creativity, curiosity and learning were embraced.

In hindsight, being aware of the religious and cultural differences of the students and being accommodating to all backgrounds and beliefs was the norm in Columbia. We learned about all the different religious holidays, decorated for all faiths during the holidays and did not sing songs with any religious lyrics. So, I guess you could say that we were allowed to speak our religious and political opinions but were expected to be "politically correct" at the same time. And at that point in time, no one even knew what being "politically correct" meant. Respecting and honoring each other was just the norm for us.

Getting ready for High School was so exciting. There was a lot of talk about wonderful Wilde Lake High School. Wilde Lake High was a more sophisticated version of the middle school architecture. As with the elementary and middle school, the Media Center was the focal point of the school. The school was round, with the Media Center on a central "level" with access from all learning areas of the school. The academic classes were a flight of steps up from the Media Center. These classes were also in large pods, rather than individual classrooms. Home room assignments were with a specific teacher within a certain team, but classes were throughout all the pods. The specialty classrooms like, music, art, home economics and shop were on the lower level of the school. The gymnasium, cafeteria, administrative offices and most of the lockers were on the lower level as well. Wilde Lake was equipped with a beautiful 800-seat auditorium with a state-of-the-art proscenium stage. The gym had great facilities as well.

Interior of an open space school in Columbia. (Photo The Rouse Company)

The media center inside Wilde Lake High School. (Photo Paul Abel)

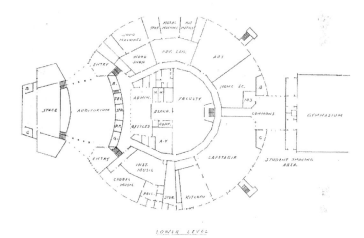

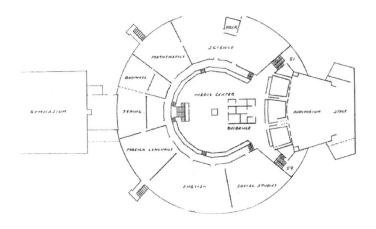

Like the primary grades, the self-paced curriculum was still in use for most classes. This new style of learning was part of the concept of the open environment that Columbia could offer. Each child could find their own path to success and was embraced as being unique and special. The belief held by the Columbia education system was that if given the opportunity to grow, to do well and to thrive, children would rise to the occasion. At Wilde Lake High School, there was no such thing as an "F" grade or "failing" a class. You just kept repeating the work until you passed. There is much merit in this approach, as it ensured that no one was considered, or felt like, a failure.

I would say that this method worked, for the most part. If you speak with people who grew up in the original Columbia school system, you will find that most are still raving about the special opportunities that were available to them. This self-paced learning environment had its share of challenges, as well as benefits. For those students, like myself, who were self-directed but lacked the discipline to take more than was necessary for graduation, we could take the classes we wanted and finish the work as we could, but there was nobody to coach us into taking more than what we needed. I graduated in the top 10% of my class, but lacked study discipline, which contributed to poor study habits in college.

For students who excelled, who were driven to a higher standard, the opportunities were pretty much endless. Many kids finished school in three rather than four years because they were able to work at their own pace and complete the required classes by the end of their Junior year. There were many advance placement classes available as well, with college credits available through the local community college. In retrospect, the program did not fare well for students who were somewhat academically challenged but who didn't need remedial or special education assistance. These students often fell through the cracks. It was not unusual for those students to take five or sometimes even six years to complete high school. However, dropout rate was extremely low. In the end, the students were not made to feel like a failure and the learning that was supposed to take place, did — even if it took extra years of school. All in all, students at Wilde Lake High School excelled.

It was obvious then, and still is today, that being a Pioneer Kid was a very special honor. Sure, there were cliques in high school and your share of outcasts, but for the most part, the "Jocks" got along with the "Nerds," who hung out with the "Drama and Music Geeks," all of whom knew but didn't shun the "Stoners." It was like one big, relatively happy, functional family. Lunch tables were filled with kids from all the different "cliques" and of all ethnic backgrounds. There was no (or very little) self-segregation. A good example of this was illustrated in the music and theater department. Football players decided it was cool to sing in the choir, march in the band and perform in the plays. All it took was one brave kid to break the mold and the rest was Columbia history.

Another example of the diversity of Columbia showed clearly in the drama school programs offered through the Columbia School of Theatrical Arts. Most notably, as the USA approached its Bi-Centennial, the schools founder, Toby Orenstein, put together two troops of performers. "The Young Columbians" and the "Junior Young Columbians," who performed all over Columbia and the Baltimore-Washington area, telling the history of our country, from 1776 to1976, through songs and dances representing the country's journey. I was fortunate enough to have attended the Columbia School of Theatrical Arts and was a member of the Junior Young Columbians. The mix of ethnicities within the group of performers shined a bright light on the importance and beauty of the diversity in people and showed how our country was founded on people of different backgrounds coming to this country to pursue freedom of religion, liberty and justice. The Young Columbians performed at the White House for President Carter and performed at Disney World in Orlando Florida. The reach of the Columbia ideal was far.

Toby Orenstein's theatrical arts school produced many talented young performers who went on to have successful Broadway, television, movie and musical theater careers. Toby opened an award-winning dinner theater in the mid-80's, Toby's Dinner Theater of Columbia, that continues to produce top-notch theater in an intimate, in-the-round setting. The Columbia Center of Theatrical Arts (CCTA) is still active and producing new talent, and there has been a recent revival of The Young Columbians. Toby has been and continues to be a pillar in the theater and arts community in Columbia and the surrounding area. A second Toby's was opened in Baltimore, Maryland.

CHAPTER 5:

Leaving the Nest

I graduated from Wilde Lake High School June 1, 1978. I was in the top 10% of my class. Which in hindsight was not difficult to do, being you couldn't fail and everyone had at least a C average. I performed in my graduation, including writing 4-part harmony to a song titled "The Apple Tree" from the 1970's Broadway musical "The Me Nobody Knows," — a beautiful song, written about having hope during times of desperation. I also performed "Color My World" by the band Chicago, accompanying myself on piano — another song about moving on and how hopes and dreams of a better tomorrow is what brings color to your world. I had decided to go on to study vocal music in college. I attended Hartt School of Music at the University of Hartford, in W. Hartford Connecticut that fall.

I was so excited to move out on my own and to experience life outside of Columbia. Things were pretty exciting in the late 70's and American culture was finding its way out of the revolution of the 60's and into an era of computer technology and a much larger presence for women in the workforce. Music during that time was so diverse, with some of the biggest names in the music industry reaching their height of popularity, such as Led Zeppelin, Pink Floyd, Queen, AC/DC, Yes, The Eagles, Earth, Wind & Fire, Sly and the Family Stone, Stevie Wonder and Parliament-Funkadelic, to name a few. Many of these artists are still performing today, and all have heavily influenced the metamorphosis of pop culture. Granted it was also the time of skin tight jeans, platform shoes, silk shirts and disco, but you've gotta take the good with the bad.

I arrived at school late in August, moved into my dorm room and started college life. The population of the school was primarily white and what students of color there were pretty much stayed to themselves. I didn't really get why everyone was separated, but it all seemed okay to me. There were mixers that everyone attended and other events on campus in which people all seemed to get along, so I went on with my life assuming people respected and honored the differences in people. Early in my sophomore year, I had friends who were juniors and seniors and lived off campus, in Hartford. I can clearly remember an evening at a local pub, where some of the kids in the neighborhood had gone out randomly slashing tires. People were pretty upset. I was in a haze of confusion, witnessing this type of hate-filled, violent exchange between the neighborhood whites at this bar, cops, and some of the local black folks. It wasn't pretty. It was there, for the first time, that I heard the "N" word used by someone. My heart sank. I couldn't believe that someone my own age, in the late 1970's, was still so prejudice and bigoted. I walked away from the conversation, primarily because I was frightened and confused, but also because I knew if I did say anything it wouldn't be in support of the victims of this crime, it would be to criticize the person for using the "N" word. Although I didn't really talk about it with any of my friends, the image I had built in my head of a world where everyone got along and people of all different backgrounds coexisted peacefully, came crashing down around me.

After that incident, my focus in life started to change. I wanted to be with friends who were open-minded, fun, free-spirited and believed in "peace, love and understanding." I found that with a very special group of friends. Although there was little diversity in the color of our skin, there was much diversity in our social and religious backgrounds and we all looked beyond those differences. We created our own culture. We were involved in social movements, peaceful demonstrations, rock-n-roll music, psychedelics, and basically, the peace, love and understanding I needed in my life at that time.

As it happens, many of these friends have remained friends for life.

Although we have all mellowed over the years, the general understanding about life, love, peace and understanding has not changed. The intellectual conversations continue, the world issues remain a focus and we continue to do the good work. Amongst this group of friends was a young man we referred to as "The A." He was a kind-hearted soul, a deep thinker, an exceptional guitarist, very intellectual, easy to look at, and at the end of my sophomore year, we were engaged to be married. We married right after school let out that year. I was 19 and he had just turned 21. He was from Concord, NH and was the son of a Congregationalist minister. Here I was, a Jewish girl from a family in this crazy little town in MD called Columbia, with a black brother and sister, marrying a minister's son. How could this story unfold? With many exciting chapters, twists and turns, well developed characters and a real continuation of the story of how James Rouse's concept for Columbia could reach outside of the town and into the lives of so many others.

My husband Steve and I had a baby shortly after our first anniversary. Both families embraced us and the new life we had begun. We were still living outside of Hartford, but both Steve and I had stopped going to school and had refocused our attention on raising a family. We decided to move to Columbia and raise our little girl in an environment where she could know peace, love and understanding. Where she could go outside and play, explore with friends of all backgrounds, and not be judged for being the daughter of a mixed-faith couple, or being a Jew. Natalie was growing up so fast. By the time she was 4, she had a sister, Leah, who was born in Columbia.

Steve and I reconnected with some of my friends from my years in Columbia and started to expand our social network. We had a band and started an independent record label. Between 1984 and 1990, we produced 5 compilation albums (3 on vinyl, 1 on cassette and one on CD) featuring various original artists from all over the world. Our band was quite diverse, so our message of honoring diversity could not only be heard, but seen. (Rachel and Henry Cross, a couple who were some of our original band members, would go on to become pillars in the music and art scene in the DC Metropolitan Area and have continued to entertain for the next 30+ years.)

We sang songs about the social and political issues of our time. We were some of the first musicians to really do multi-media productions. Images were projected on the screen behind the band that correlated with our message. We produced two "rock operas" and even had the

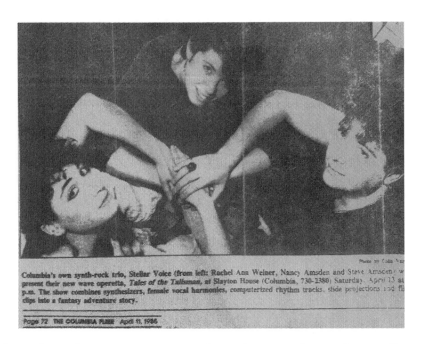

Columbia's own synth-rock trio, Stellar Voice (from left: Rachel Ann Weiner, Nancy Amsden and Steve Amsden) w present their new wave operetta, Tales of the Talisman, at Slayton House (Columbia, 730-2380) Saturday April 13 at p.m. The show combines synthesizers, female vocal harmonies, computerized rhythm tracks, slide projections and fi clips into a fantasy adventure story.

Page 72 THE COLUMBIA FLIER April 11, 1985

local modern dance company perform in one of our shows. Some of our more popular songs were, "Living in the Now," "In Between the Lines," and "Rust on the Iron Curtain." During this period of time, our extended family became more diverse as well. My brother Sam met and married a nice Catholic girl, from Albany, New York. He met her while flying kites on the beach. One of my cousins married a black man and started a family. We were living a life of meaning and with purpose.

Columbia was a great place to raise our kids. Our circle of friends was as diverse as could be, and our children were exposed to so many wonderful cultural experiences. Our music reached a broad audience and our girls were being raised in an environment full of love, laughter, music and song. They played on the floor in the "band room" and often came with us to gigs. I was also the music director at the Howard County Jewish Community School and taught music to children from preschool to 12th grade. The music came from Jewish folk music, religious text and folk songs about social justice, peace, love and understanding. Steve worked for various tech companies and helped provide the final foundation we needed to continue our music, start our recording company and live the life we desired, which included traveling and experiencing as much culture and adventure that we could.

CHAPTER 6:

The Great White North

In 1988, money was tight and work was not producing what it needed to in order to continue raising our family the way we wanted to. Steve took a job working for his father's surveying company in New Hampshire and we made the move out of Columbia. Moving to Concord, NH, a community, and state for that matter, that is predominantly white, Christian and conservative, was a real culture shock for me. But Steve's family was there and they were wonderful. I always felt welcome and I knew my daughters would be loved unconditionally. The air there was clean; there was plenty of "open space" for the girls to play, and life in NH, although pretty "white bread," would be a great place to raise our kids. There was also much more opportunity in NH to live in the country, which was very appealing to Steve, away from commotion of suburban or urban life. Although it took some time for me to get used to it, I grew to love the solitude and quiet. It was a different kind of peace, love and understanding, and I embraced it.

Living in New Hampshire certainly had its challenges. We were so far away from my family and from the lifestyle of Columbia. Special family events often took place in a church and any non-Christian (or non-New England) culture I wanted for my family, I had to create in my home. There were very few Jews in the area and the very small synagogue in town was Conservative, which I was not at all accustomed to nor interested in. This was a challenge I took on whole-heartedly. Steve and I always wanted the girls to learn about the traditions and values from both of our families, so we celebrated

"Christmakah," or "Hannumas," and "Bunnyover." We had Steve's family over for all of our celebrations and over the years they all learned my Jewish traditions and I learned theirs. These were always joyous occasions. The best was hearing Steve's dad say Hebrew words with a Yankee accent.

At that time, in the 1990's, there was a growing awareness of the need for cultural diversity in the workplace. Diversity Management programs were more common in the culturally astute cities on the East Coast and other culturally diverse areas of business and industry throughout the country. It was a change very different than the Affirmative Action programs introduced throughout the previous three decades. It wasn't just about equal opportunity; there was a new understanding, a corporate value, that inclusion and cultural awareness strengthened a company in both the job satisfaction of its employees as well as its marketability and strength in the industry. Those companies that didn't embrace a corporate culture of diversity awareness could no longer survive in a diverse market. New Hampshire did not have a diverse population, and at the time I started working, companies in the area were yet to embrace this new way of operating.

I began working in the insurance industry, in the consumer service division of a large health insurance company. This required a great deal of adjustment for me. My only work experience had been music, waiting tables and raising my children. This corporate job felt very foreign to me and I couldn't have put myself in a more conservative work environment. However, I discovered early on that the executive management team of this company didn't only "talk" about diversity, they walked the walk. They recognized the value of having a diverse workforce and the importance of attracting and maintaining talent from a diverse pool. Over the 15 years I worked for this company, I saw the workforce becoming more diverse. After some major "culture shifts" in the company, they began a diversity management program. The passion I was looking for in my job was found. I volunteered for and was selected to sit on the first Regional Diversity Council. This was a national company with offices in 47 states and their Diversity Initiative was serious business. I served for two years on the council.

The late 1990's and early 2000's brought about a lot of changes in the way that companies in NH did business. I was witness to a cultural shift in my own company, but I also saw that change in many of the large corporations in the state. I did hear some complaining out in the community that Boston Massachusetts was encroaching on the culture of New Hampshire and that the peace and solitude that New Hampshire embraced was going to go by the wayside. New Hampshire is the "Live Free or Die" state. Many people believed all of "these people" (diverse people) coming from other states were going to ruin that. I remember an onslaught of bumper stickers that read, "Welcome to NH... now go home," but I didn't take much notice of this. I welcomed the migration of a more diverse population into New Hampshire. I saw these changes as the beginning of a new era and I truly felt that I had made a difference. Had I not grown up "Columbia" I may not have had the interest or drive to become an integral part of the cultural paradigm shift. Taking part in this shift was so rewarding. Communities and companies in NH who embraced the need for diversity were able to ride the crest of a new age in business and helped to build the infrastructure and provide more jobs. This change in business culture helped to attract more business and a more diverse population to an area that had only a few years previously been predominantly white.

My husband and I attempted to continue with our independent record label and promotion and production company, looking for artists in New England for live events. Trying to break into the Boston area music scene proved more difficult than we had anticipated. Boston was not a great area for budding original artists. We also found the commute to the city too difficult, and our children were getting older and our time was more occupied with school events and sleepover parties. We did get together a new band and played in clubs, at parties and held a few events. We were even the guest artists for the Libertarian Party NH Convention. Now THAT was quite an experience!

We purchased our first home in NH, with the help of Steve's parents. It was a passive solar, berm house on about 3 acres. It was very cool having a berm house. It was small, only 800 square feet, but it was perfect for our first home. We had another band and we practiced in the garage. We got our first dog, first kitten and then 2 more dogs. We were living the life. We even had some ducks and chickens. We loved spending time with Steve's family, and he reconnected with a few friends he knew when he was growing up. I got very close with my mother-in-law over the years. She was a loving and accepting woman and we enjoyed our time together. We learned a lot from each other as we got to know more about the different backgrounds and environments from which we came.

As we settled into this new environment, we decided that we needed to find a community that could provide a place to meet with other like-minded people, where our children could be exposed to other cultures. We decided to connect with the Unitarian Universalist Church of Concord. This seemed to be a good place for us. Although there wasn't any real diversity represented in the congregants, there was an embracing and inclusion of many different belief systems and traditions. The congregation recognized all the different holidays from many different faiths and celebrated the most important holidays for the more prevalent religions. We could attend a Christmas service, a Rosh Hashanah service, as well as a service recognizing the solstice and equinox. This was also a "Welcoming" church. It was a place where same sex couples and mixed race or mixed religion couples and their families could come to gather together for fellowship. The motto for the church was, "Where we honor the worth and dignity of all peoples." This rang true for us, and so we remained connected to the UUC for our years in New Hampshire.

We soon outgrew the little berm house and purchased a 4 bedroom colonial in the outskirts of Concord. This got the kids into the Concord school system, which provided a much better high school environment than what would have been had we stayed in the first house. The house was closer to Steve's family's "camp," which was a real bonus. We moved there when Natalie was in 8th grade. We drove her back and forth to school so she wouldn't have to change schools in the middle of the last year of middle-school.

As our girls became young women, a tradition in my religion was to be Bat Mitzvah. This was a ceremony where, at 13, a young man or woman would speak before the congregation about their understanding of God and life, as they are welcomed into the congregation as an adult member. We wanted our girls to have this type of celebration of their coming of age. The UUC was able to accommodate us. Being the unconventional people that we were, and having children who also thought unconventionally, our girls decided to have "Art" Mitzvahs. Natalie had a little ceremony at home where she welcomed family and friends, read something she had written and decorated a wall in our family room with all of her artwork she had created from when she was very small until her most current pieces. Natalie never really had the desire to have any religious symbolism in her celebration, but she did like the idea of presenting herself to our community as an adult. Leah had more connection to her Jewish heritage and enjoyed the community of the church setting. Her "Art" Mitzvah was held in the chapel at the church. She wrote a song about life and performed it, had readings by family members, read a chapter of the Old Testament and gave a speech about what it meant to her. Leah's event was much more like a traditional Bat Mitzvah, but with her own twist. Both families attended both special events and were so supportive of how Steve and I were choosing to provide faith to our children.

Through our association with the Concord UUC, we got to know several community leaders, and for the holidays in 1998 we were asked if we were interested in being featured in an article in the Concord Monitor, talking about how families with mixed faith backgrounds celebrate. This was front page news for Concord. During the years that we lived there, we witnessed a shift in the population and the way of thinking of this community. Slowly, more people of color decided to make central NH their home. Although still a very small percentage of the population, it was evident that people of different backgrounds were feeling more comfortable with moving to the area, as they were much more welcomed. For a state that, in 1988, was still very conservative and the population still quite "old", in 1998, a new migration of younger and more diverse families was moving north, to take advantage of the beautiful scenery, clean air and open spaces. In the last few years we were in New Hampshire, the state elected a Democratic, female Governor and the once very RED state, started to change to Purple. Traditional values still hold firm in New Hampshire, which is part of its charm. It is unlikely it will ever be a liberal BLUE state, but Steve and I like to think that our influence in the community might actually have had an effect.

Our oldest daughter met a young man late in her senior year of high school, whom she later married. He was a nice Catholic boy, which added a new dynamic to our multi-religious family. Natalie would joke that she couldn't have met a guy any more "White" than her boyfriend. He even had a very "White" name: Robert Michael Smith. She was right; you couldn't get any more "white" than that.

Right after Natalie graduated from high school, we sold our home and moved to a small duplex we purchased as an investment property while we were waiting for our "dream house" to be built on the banks of the Blackwater River, a small, class A river in central NH, on which Steve's family had built their "camp." We loved this magical place, ringed with huge white pines that had originally been part of the King of England's mast yard. We always said that if the piece of land at the entrance to the right-of-way were ever for sale, we wanted to buy it and build. Just by chance, we discovered that the owner was considering selling it and we contacted him. Next thing you know, we were selling our nice 4-bedroom colonial and were building a chalet style home on a 7 acre parcel with 800' of water frontage.

From November until April 1st the entire family worked on finishing the house. The house was a modified cape with floor to 28' ceiling windows. Only the first floor was "finished" and we did all the rest: taping and mudding the main floor, hanging drywall, painting the entire house (including the high, vaulted ceilings, which Natalie did, like a monkey on a ladder), finishing the upstairs, which included two small bedrooms and a loft, and sanding and finishing the wood floors. It was a very snowy winter that year, so we were snow blowing our way into the house to work on it and snow blowing our way back out (well, Steve was doing the snow blowing). It was a labor of family love, and we adored our house on the Blackwater River.

During that crazy time where we were building our house and getting settled, my mother had been dealing with her second battle with breast cancer. She would live with the disease for nearly 13 years.

Leah had the privilege of attending Hopkinton High School. It was the finest public high school in the state of NH. Hopkinton was fairly affluent and, being a small town of about 9,000, the middle and high schools were together in one building. There were 800 students in grades 6-12. Leah's graduating class had less than 100 students. Many of Leah's friends, including her first love, were exchange students—not surprisingly. My girls had a tendency to be drawn to peers who were of differing ethnicities, as the cultural diversity seemed normal and appealing to them. Natalie attended a larger high school of 2,000 students, only about 2-5 percent being non-white—nearly all of which being in her group of friends. Even in an environment of very little diversity, both of my children sought out the enriching life experience of embracing those who are different from themselves.

At that time, we could not foresee that the river of our lives, as a family, would soon be taking many curves, and forking in new directions.

CHAPTER 7:

Heading Down to Dixie

In 2003-2004, our youngest daughter's senior year in high school, our family began a slow migration to Florida. Leah had decided that she was tired of living in the "great white north" and wanted to go to college in Florida. She narrowed down her schools and selected a small Catholic university in horse country of West Central Florida. We had never seen this part of Florida and really enjoyed our visit while we were looking at schools. It was late in the fall of 2003, and while NH was suffering its first snowfall, we were exploring Clearwater Beach and enjoying the sunshine and 80-degree weather. There was the occasional chatter about wanting to go away to Florida with Leah. We could all go back to college. After a successful trip and the selection of the school, we flew home to New Hampshire. We were welcomed by brown grass, leafless trees and gray skies. We were not ready to be home. We shared our stories with our older daughter, about the palm trees, the warm weather and our trip to the beach. She got a glazed look in her eyes.

That winter was a particularly cold one. A "cold spell" of 20 days, with nighttime temperatures below zero and daytime temps not getting above 15 degrees, made the winter seem endless. There was a blizzard in March that year. At the end of that blizzard, our oldest announced that she and Robert were quitting their jobs and were moving to the Orlando, Florida area. They sold almost everything and moved to Florida the 1st of April. Who's the April fool there? I think it was those staying behind in what felt like the arctic tundra.

That June, our youngest was graduating high school. Her sister was planning to come up for graduation and it didn't take long for them to scheme about Leah heading to Florida before the start of college. So, graduation came and went and Leah went down to live with Natalie and her husband for the summer, before starting college in August. It seemed to be in a blink of an eye that I went from "active parenting" to being an empty-nester. Over that summer, Leah met a young man who would later become her husband. Victor was originally from Puerto Rico and was living and working in the Orlando area. Leah started school in August. and every weekend for the next year, Victor traveled the two-hour trip to pick up or visit with Leah and make the two-hour trip back. It often meant 4 two-hour trips in 3 days. It was true love for sure. The next year Leah transferred to UCF, just outside of Orlando, and moved in with her sister.

That year was rough for me. A visit to Florida and a couple holiday visits from the girls just wasn't enough. I think Steve sensed that I needed to be in Florida with my daughters.

I lost my dad that winter. He had been fighting cancer and had taken a fall on the ice out in front of the house. His body was weakened from the chemo, and although he was recovering from the therapy, the fall was more than his body could handle. I had a very strong internal calling telling me that I needed to go see my Dad. He was being moved from the general hospital into a rehab facility. I flew down to see him. It was hard seeing him in such a weakened state — not able to feed himself or get out of bed without help. He was always such a strong and independent man. I think losing his ability to take care of himself also took its toll.

Before I left, he had asked my mom to bring his sweat suit from home so he could start his physical therapy. He seemed to have a bit more will and strength than when I had gotten there, so I headed home. I got the call the next morning that he had passed overnight. It was as if I had Divine guidance to go and see him and that he was waiting until he had seen me.

At this point, Steve was unhappy in his job and just couldn't deal with the high tech life at work, when it was the gypsy lifestyle he craved. He started looking for work in Florida. I didn't think he was really serious, but certainly didn't try to persuade him otherwise. One evening he came to me and said he was going to fly to Florida to check out a job working as a farmhand on a bamboo plantation. He showed me the ad he had answered. This bamboo farm was looking for a farmhand to work about 20 hours a week in exchange for a place to live, on or near the farm and a small stipend. In the ad it said, "must be comfortable with nudity." Seemed odd to me, but I was not too concerned about what this could mean.

Steve went down to Florida to meet with the owners of this bamboo plantation. They put him to work for a day and he reported back that he really liked it and was going to take the job. He was going to come home, get some of our stuff packed and drive back down in two weeks. Then he mentioned that the owners of this bamboo farm were nudists. I'm all about diversity, but this was a bit outside of my comfort zone. But it was a way for us to get to Florida, to be closer to the girls and to get out of the cold and frosty lifestyle that is New Hampshire.

We planned to have Steve work in Florida for one month before I would join him. He would fly up to New Hampshire, along with the girls and their guys, and we would have one last New Hampshire style family vacation, which we did in Cape Cod, Massachusetts. We were joined by Steve's parents, as well as my mom and my niece Jasmine. It was a great vacation. When we got back, we would pack the moving truck and Steve and I would make the move. The girls and their guys would all fly back to Florida. During the last evening together as a family in New Hampshire, in our empty home and the furniture waiting on the truck, Victor proposed to Leah with all the family there to witness. It was a wonderful ending to that chapter of our lives.

Over the next year or so, Steve's vision of his future as an empty-nester became very different than mine. He was talking about dealing antiques and refinishing furniture and traveling between FL and NH in a van. I was more interested in a house near a beach or lake and a Class A motor home. We were drifting apart, but I didn't see it.

Our first year in Florida was really culture shock for me. It wasn't until I was in the south that I realized what a "Yankee" I was. The bamboo farm was in a little town about 30 miles north of Orlando. I took a part-time job waiting tables at a Cracker Barrel. Unlike many areas of Florida, where most residents were "transplants" or "snow birds," Clermont was a real little southern town. Outdoor country music festivals, huge flea markets and corn festivals were all that were offered for cultural activities. That first fall we went to an outdoor country music festival and on the entry sign it read, "No Glass, No Alcohol, No Dogs and No Firearms." I was not in Kansas anymore, Toto! After a few months I took a job working for the Florida Department of Insurance as a specialist on the department's insurance hotline.

My first real "learnin'" about the culture of the deep south was when I took a trip to Tallahassee for a week of training. I was paired up with a woman from Pensacola. I always referred to that area of Florida as "South Louisiana." The culture of the panhandle of Florida is much more like the deep south than the Orlando area. She was a nice person, intelligent and seemed pretty open-minded. We shared about our lives, and I learned that she was the daughter of a family that had owned a plantation. Her great, great grandparents were slave owners. I felt like I was in the Twilight Zone. Her father and brothers were still quite prejudice, although she did not feel that way herself. She explained how her family had a deep love for the family that was formerly their plantation slaves. Over the years, the family that had been slaves on that plantation stayed and worked for her family, by "choice." Initially they were indentured but were freed, paid a wage and provided a home on the grounds. The children all played together and eventually went to school together. Despite the change in relationship and fondness for the servant family, her father and brothers (and other family elders) never saw their black neighbors and employees as equals. Slang was still used in reference to them, even though they often had meals together, socialized and attended each others' family events, like weddings and funerals.

We talked about why there was a distrust and hatred of "Yankees" in the south. She explained that folks from the north looked down on southerners, regardless of how they may have changed their attitudes toward people of color. She said, "Yankees don't want us to remember or acknowledge our heritage and history." I had never thought about it that way. It was time for me to expand my mind and let in the southerner's history and try to understand why they feel differently about black people. I didn't have to like it, and

I clearly still felt that it was time for them to let go of their narrow and bigoted point of view. However, I had a better understanding of why they felt and acted the way they did. Could I find room in my life for this type of thinking? I still was not sure.

That "huge flea market" I mentioned earlier was the site of my second lesson in tolerance for intolerance. It manifested while getting to know some of the people who made their living working at Renninger's Flea Market in Mount Dora, Florida. Steve began to collect used furniture, "tchotchkes" and antiques and sell it at this giant flea market. He met and befriended an interesting group of "junk heads," as I like to call them. Every weekend was spent with these people. I went with Steve some weekends and hung out with this group of southern folk; they were uneducated, bigoted, gun-toting rednecks. There was one man who seemed out of place; a young, hippie-type man who seemed to have an outlook on life much more like Steve and I did. I felt so out of place there.

One of Steve's friends really stood out to me. I really had no idea how to relate to him. I did see some endearing qualities, including making the best collard greens and ham hocks I had ever eaten, and Steve seemed to really like him. Racist slang words were thrown around freely, but I just tried to remember what my roommate in Tallahassee told me and to find a place of understanding. I did admire that this man lived "off the grid," way out in the country. He grew his own food and generated his own electricity. That was pretty cool and very resourceful. One evening Steve and I were invited over to his friend's house for dinner. We drove way out into the country, down dirt roads, across fields and into the woods. It was really a sight to see this hand-built house with the farm animals, hunting dogs in runs out back, gardens and a big, old, propane powered generator. Man, did that thing make a racket! He had captured a wild boar that had been marauding his animals and garden, which he was keeping in a pen until it came time to have a pig roast.

Then, we went inside. The rooms were dark, with high, slanted ceilings. The cabinets and wood- work were dark and it made me feel very closed in. Hanging on the wall over the dining table was a big confederate flag. A shelf in the kitchen was home to a collection of "Aunt Jemima" type dolls; "Mammies" is what he called them. I wasn't sure how to react. We sat down at the table, and before we ate, we all said grace. I had eaten with many families and friends who said grace before meals, but this time I really felt uncomfortable. Did he know I was a Jew? How would he react if he knew?

I decided to do a little probing to see about his history and learn about his family. Perhaps I could find a way to deal with all of this by understanding it better. So, I asked him about his collection and what significance these items had to him. He explained that he came from a fairly wealthy, old Florida family. He was raised by his family's "Mammie." He spoke of her with such love. I could tell that she took very good care of him and he truly loved her. Yet the "N" word was used several times in his story.

I have to admit that I did come away from that evening with more of an understanding of why he was the way that he was. I also came away with the realization that I did not have room in my life for people who believed the way he did about people who weren't white. Knowing that my husband had become so entrenched in this flea market lifestyle, was able to blend in with this crowd and really seemed to like them and their lifestyle, was the first real sign that I could no longer live in this world that we had created.

I never believed for a minute that Steve subscribed to this narrow way of thinking. He was an open-minded, fair and just person. He didn't have a prejudiced bone in his body. But the fact that he could find a way to fit into that world was just too far out of my realm of understanding. Over the next 8 months, our marriage came to an end. In time, he did find a way to live the life he wanted; doing his antique and used furniture collecting getting a place out in the boonies where he could raise his chickens and live a very simple life. He left the Renninger's Flea Market world and moved on with his life; coming to a place that is much more suited to the man I had spent 27 years with. We are still friends to this day and share many of our family holidays and special events together with the entire family. I am grateful for that.

2008 brought about many changes. There were some hard times, adjusting to being single. I lived with Natalie and her husband, as well as Leah and Victor. Natalie and Robert were also drifting apart and within only a matter of months, she too had left her marriage.

She was going through a real metamorphosis, a transformation, which we will talk about in a future chapter. I too was beginning my metamorphosis. I started eating healthier and took a much healthier attitude about life. I benefited from a friendship with a young man I worked with who had really mastered living life with positive intention. I learned a lot from him. I also started losing weight. In the next six months I lost a total of 65 pounds. There were definitely lessons to be learned about living "large."

In the midst of all of this marriage ending turmoil, Leah was planning her wedding. Leah and Victor married that spring. The wedding was, as is traditional in our family, full of different ethnic traditions. Steve's father (Congregational Minister) performed the ceremony, I sang both in English and in Hebrew, we combined the Jewish and Christian traditions and now were including some of Victor's family traditions. Some of Victor's family from Puerto Rico came to join us for the celebration and our family expanded its horizons once again.

These were very emotional times for all of us, but we are a strong and close family and have all come through it and are in a better and happier place. Also, during this year of change, I was laid off from my job with the State. I took a job with an outsourcing company and was laid off from that job five months later. The Florida economy, along with the rest of the country, was crashing. By the end of that year, Natalie sold her house, and I found myself jobless and homeless. (Well, never REALLY homeless.)

Finding myself and my dog, Jack, without a real place to live, no work and no prospects, I was living a life of uncertainty. Interestingly enough, I was not agitated or depressed. Over the past several months I had gone through a real transformation. Only a few weeks after Steve and I split, I felt as though I had sprouted wings. I started on a path of rediscovery and, let's call it, enlightenment.

I read the book *The Power of Now* by Eckhart Tolle, on the recommendation of Natalie. Shortly after, Natalie, Leah, Victor and I all participated in *A New Earth* webcast with Oprah Winfrey and Eckhart Tolle. It was an amazing experience. The first night of the webinar, covering Chapter 1, tens of thousands of participants were expected and nearly 500,000 people attempted to log on at the same time. The system was not able to handle the traffic, so there were problems with the transmission and many couldn't get on the call. Oprah advised that they would fix this problem and do the first chapter again the following day. The power of so many people, all over the world, coming together for a potentially life-changing learning experience was, well, life changing. Millions of people all over the world have now viewed the webcast.

That course put me on a path of knowledge and understanding that has helped me to rediscover my center, my personal vortex, my spiritual self. So, when I found myself a drifter on the sea of uncertainty, the waters were calm.

During this time, my mom was nearing the end of her battle with cancer. The message was clear. With no job and no stable place to live, I was to head home to spend time with my mom, during her last days on this earth.

CHAPTER 8:

Back to the Nest, Then Fly South Again

Moving back to Columbia was like looking toward endings and beginnings. My mom was living in the house that she and my dad had built in 1982. The Allen Homes house was a contemporary with redwood siding, cathedral ceilings, open staircase, 4 bedrooms, 3 baths and eventually, an apartment in the basement. Allen Homes became one of the most popular builders in Columbia. The modern architecture and natural wood siding blended so nicely into the park and tree lined communities.

My mom lived alone in the house for the five years after my father passed away. With the loss of two jobs leaving me in limbo, it was the perfect opportunity to spend quality time with my mom. She was not doing well. Two runs with breast cancer over 12 years had taken its toll on her body. The cancer had metastasized and was pretty much everywhere in her body. Frail, weak and thin, my mom still had the fight of a warrior. Her spirit and will to be alive and vibrant gave her the strength to live with cancer for so many years. She lived for her family. Her children, grandchildren, family and friends were her strength. I often thought that she didn't look out for herself, but for my mom, looking out for others was what she lived for.

Although this would come to be known as "The Family House," it was never my home. It felt foreign to me, as it had been built after I was already in college. Over the years, Steve, Natalie, Leah and I had come to this house to visit for holidays, family dinners, special occasions, welcoming new members of the family, weddings, bar mitzvah and memorial services.

My parents continued to be pillars in the Columbia community. Over the years, new faces joined the circle, and many of those original, Pioneer families continued to share in life's special and sacred moments. Our Rabbi, Martin Siegel of the "Innovative" Columbia Jewish Congregation, officiated for our family milestones and supported our family and the diversity and values that we embraced. Rabbi Siegel and his wife also adopted a multi-racial child a few years after my sister joined our family.

Natalie and I loaded up my VW wagon with as much stuff as could fit, including my dog, Jack, and made the 15-hour drive from FL to MD. I was so grateful that Natalie was willing to travel along to share the driving and keep me company. Driving Interstate 95 for 15 hours can be pretty monotonous. I left most of my things in storage down in Florida and intended to officially move it up to Maryland once I had settled in and my divorce was final. We moved over Labor Day weekend. We arrived at my mom's and settled in. It was hard to see her in such a weakened state. I know it was very uncomfortable for her to feel so helpless and vulnerable.

Natalie always had this very special connection with my mom and soon had both mom and I feeling content and just enjoying each other's company. Natalie stayed for about a week. We split our time between staying with my mom and with long-time friend, Judi. Judi had a wonderful home out in the country, about a half an hour from Columbia, and her home provided me the respite that I needed.

Shortly after Natalie headed back to Florida, my mom took a turn for the worse and we got hospice care to come to the house. Mom was still fighting the inevitable and talking with the doctors about the next treatment plan. Over the next couple of weeks, I had time to reflect on all the years in my unique family and realized what a cynic I had become. After living so many years away from my parents, my observations of them and how they raised my youngest brother and sister took on a new perspective. It seemed to me that the fact that my siblings were "different" created within my parents, especially my mother, a need to shelter them from the fact that they were different. Yet at the same time, by sheltering them it made those differences more apparent. I don't think there was ever any "prejudice" to the color of their skin, but, in hindsight, I remember hearing statements that brought this to light. As an example, I can remember my brother, as a baby, being referred to as a "brown little bean." Referring to skin color was an identifying factor in conversation and description of the family. Personally, I never understood why this differentiation was necessary. Would this make Matt and Rachel feel out of place or "different" than the rest of the family? Would it make them feel special or entitled? I started asking myself, "Did my parents really get it?"

Through this debate with myself I did come to the conclusion that they certainly *did* "get it." I grew to understand that, even with every intension of allowing no barriers and embracing diversity, it is near impossible not to identify people by their appearance. The key is, do you marvel at what makes a person who they are, or do you allow those differences to create barriers? For my parents, it was always embracing.

Mom stayed with in-home hospice only for a few days and it became quickly evident that Matt, Rachel and I were not equipped to take care of my mom and that she needed to be in the hospice home. We moved her to a beautiful hospice home with caring and respectful personnel. We knew she would be comfortable and cared for. I called my brother, Sam, and Natalie and they both flew up to spend these last days with mom. The outpouring of love and support from family and friends was astounding. The reach of my mother's love was boundless. Her lifelong friends came to spend time with her and all offered their support to my family. Even in the hospice bed, my mom was fighting, asking her oncologist for the next type of chemo. A truly remarkable woman.

Mom was in hospice less than a week when she passed. All those she touched in life were there for her in the end and showed our family just how much she meant to her family and friends and to her community, Columbia.

Still unemployed, I used the time following my mom's passing to regroup, review where I was in my life and decide what I wanted for my future. I also took time to indulge myself a little for some much needed respite, taking a 10-day trip to Hawaii with my good friend, Judi. We soaked in the sun, the culture of Hawaii, its history, the mountains, the sea, the beautiful flowers and delicious food (except

Poi—that was gross). It was the rest and relaxation that I had needed so much at that time. While I was in Hawaii, I got the call that I had a new job. I would be working for another insurance company in the legal department, where I would be responsible for reviewing new state health insurance laws and would become well versed in the implementation of the Affordable Care Act (Obamacare.) I moved out of my mom's house to an apartment in Takoma Park, MD, an eclectic and quaint little town right outside of D.C.

Takoma Park had so much to offer. Close proximity to D.C. was a huge factor in choosing Takoma Park. Great public transportation, a metro stop, shopping, a variety of ethnic restaurants and grocery stores and the human diversity I so desired. Rachel and Henry (I spoke of them earlier, in chapter 5) lived in Takoma Park and were very involved in both the music and art communities in the DC area. Their circle was very diverse and being closer to them was a wonderful experience for me. After 18 years in New Hampshire, being in the center of this cultural mecca was just what I needed.

I frequently went into DC, caught concerts and art shows, went to museums, got to visit with friends and family and really embed myself in the DC lifestyle. Leah and Victor moved to MD around the same time I did. During this time, Leah started exploring her Jewish heritage and, for a period of time, became involved with the Baltimore area Orthodox community. It was difficult for Leah and Victor, being that Victor is not Jewish. In the Orthodox community, interfaith marriages were not readily accepted. The community liked Victor (what's not to like?) but they didn't "recognize" their marriage. Over the next couple of years, the two found a way to incorporate some of the traditional Orthodox practices without compromising their union. It was a very interesting time for all of us.

Even though I was brought up in a Jewish home, we were far from traditional. We didn't keep kosher (bacon, sausage, shell fish and cheeseburgers were regular faire in our house), and we didn't dress conservatively or observe a traditional Sabbath. Leah's exploration of her Jewish roots helped us all to learn and grow. During the last year in MD, Leah, Victor and I shared a home in Baltimore County. Takoma Park was a very expensive place to live and sharing a house made having a bigger home possible.

Although there were so many wonderful opportunities available to us in Maryland, we all felt the pull to go back to Florida. Leah and Victor did not feel attached to their local jobs, and by my third year in Maryland I was working from home full time. Making the move seemed like a good idea. Before I moved in with Leah and Victor, I had looked at buying a small condo in Takoma Park. A 650 square foot apartment was going for $225K. Yikes. I started looking at properties in Florida, in the area that Natalie was living, near Clearwater Beach in Pinellas County, just north of Tampa on the Gulf of Mexico. I found that I could buy an entire house for half the cost of the condo. Having my family together, by the beach, where the weather was always nice, was extremely appealing.

Steve had moved back to Florida also, so he too would be able to have his girls close, and we could share family events and holidays together. I went down to Florida the beginning of July 2013, looking for a house. I gave myself 2 weeks to look. I found a nice 3 bed 2 bath, Florida-style ranch house 1.5 miles from the beach, in a lovely little town called Tarpon Springs. Tarpon Springs is a primarily Greek community and a fishing village, known for the sponge diving industry, great Greek food and culture, a thriving art community and the "Old Florida" flavor that northern Pinellas County is famous for. I made the move the middle of September. Leah and Victor found an apartment near the University of Southern Florida, in Tampa, where she would finish her degree. We would all be living no more than an hour apart.

Back to the Sunshine State

There were so many positive factors to moving back to Florida. Of course, it was very difficult leaving two of my best friends and two of my siblings, but I knew that Tarpon Springs was my life destination. About 15 years previously, Steve and I had gone to Tarpon Springs and loved it. I had said during our first visit there, "This town is so beautiful. I'd love to own a house here someday." Little did I know that I would be divorced and buying a house on my own, right in the little town that spoke to me that many years ago.

Another draw to the area was the spiritual community that exists in and around Tampa Bay. Natalie and her then boyfriend, Joeel, had built a business around living an enlightened life and transforming yourself to become the person you were destined to be. They originally worked in the area of life coaching but soon ventured into publishing. They began a magazine called "Transformation Magazine," which began as a free, local publication that focused on personal transformation and was financed and supported through advertising by businesses in the area that catered to the transformation movement. There was a need and a niche, and so they saw it and they took it. This magazine created a spiritual movement in the area and brought together many like-minded people, including alternative medicine practitioners, authors, musicians and entertainers and ultimately formed a community that I could just drop myself into when I made the move to Florida. How wonderful for me!

Part of my new community included Natalie's life partner Joeel and his family. As seemed to be the trend in my family, Natalie's partner was Puerto Rican, like Leah's husband. And he has a wonderful, loving, fun, festive and culturally rich family who has welcomed Natalie's family with open arms. Joeel has a daughter from a previous marriage who has become a wonderful addition to our extended family. I met her when I first visited with Natalie and Joeel when I was still living in MD. I called her my "Pseudo-Granddaughter." Natalie and Joeel were married in June 2014, so now I have a "real" granddaughter. Life is good!

Since the start-up of Transformation Magazine, Natalie and Joeel's business has grown and now includes Transformation Publishing, public speaking engagements, two compilation books in a "Transform Your Life" book series, which include chapters written by various authors speaking about real life experiences of transformation and growth. I have a chapter on diversity and about the Columbia experience included in "Book 2." My chapter is titled "The Grand Social Experiment." The magazine transitioned to the digital world and is now available online and through tablets and apps and is read by thousands of subscribers from all over the world. Transformation Services, Inc. is also offering on-line classes for those seeking to transform their lives.

In my job, I have continued to involve myself in Diversity Management and Corporate Culture initiatives. As was the case with my previous employer over a decade ago, this organization sees that having a diverse workforce and acknowledging and embracing the different cultures that make up the employee base speaks louder than any affirmative action requirements. These initiatives bring employees together and foster a stronger commitment to teamwork. Especially in a health insurance company, it is important for the organization to understand and address their customers' culturally diverse needs. In diversity management, when the faces of your executives, as well as your workforce, look like the consumers that you serve, you as an organization, stand out amongst your peers. I am an active member of the Corporate Culture Team for my department and have participated on the Cultural Awareness committee. I am a "Culture Ambassador" for the company and have a seat on the National Legal, Compliance and Regulatory Affairs Diversity Committee. I spend more than half of my waking hours at work and do what I can to keep the spotlight on these important company missions.

So, moving back to Florida truly has been the right move for me. I felt "called" back, even though I did not yet know for what purpose. I did know, however, that it would be here that I would find my purpose. I involved myself in this community of people full of life and spiritual awareness and was welcomed into a new family with rich cultures to share. As I acclimated to my new life, I was shown many signs that my purpose in life was to share my experience growing up in Columbia, my view on the importance of diversity in our lives and how powerful diversity management can be for all "persons" both human and corporate.

I had met with an "Intuitive" (several actually), each illuminating the idea of creating something with my hands or writing something; each lighting my path toward being a teacher and a guide and helping future generations to become all that we, as humans, are meant to be. At first these "visions" seemed unclear to me, but they all were pointing toward my greater purpose. When one intuitive told me I was going to write a book, it all clicked. I was to share my life experiences through literary platforms.

> *"I am not color-blind. My eyes are open and in awe of the*
> *rainbow of possibilities that is the human race."*
> *~Nancy Selig Amsden*

CHAPTER 9:
Carrying the Torch into the Future

As I complete the final steps of this book, I realize how timely its release is, as Columbia is celebrating its 50th birthday in 2017. This book truly celebrates the community and people that Columbia has produced. I use the word "produced" to illustrate the years of planning, implementation, growth and refinement that has gone into producing the "products" of Columbia — the people who grew up there who have grown to become some of the most worldly, open-minded, accepting people on this planet (at least in my opinion). I have often referred to myself as a "Product of Columbia"; a statement filled with pride and endearment for the community and its people, whom have helped to shape the woman that I am today. I imagine those of you reading this book, who have experienced living in Columbia, feel the same way.

This book also celebrates Columbia's model suburban community design, the economic and social benefits of which have stood the test of time. I am not alone in praising Columbia. In fact, Money Magazine selected Columbia as the number one small city in its "Best Places to Live in 2016," citing reasons including: ranking in the top 5% for job growth, a 3.5% unemployment rate, top ranking schools, and socioeconomic, religious and racial diversity (55% white, 25% black, 12% Asian, and 8% Latino). After 50 years, Columbia is being acknowledged for being a community in which diversity is not only tolerated, it is celebrated.

At the same time, our world is on the brink of some major shifts in our humanity. On one hand we're experiencing a shift in universal consciousness and freedom of the human spirit, while on the other hand we see a rise in awareness that we still face prejudice and ignorance, violence and oppression. The outcomes future generations will inherit will be determined by the perspectives actions we take today and whether we are to continue to progress toward a nation and a world that embody the ideals that Columbia represents.

The phrase "you must be the change you want to see in the world" (Mahatma Gandhi) could not hold more importance than it does right now. We have a responsibility to shine our light on the rest of the world, that "Every man 'neath his vine and fig tree, shall live in peace and unafraid. And into plowshares beat his sword. Nations shall study war no more" (Vine and Fig Tree). We have an opportunity to express the words, "Come on people now, shine on your brother. Everybody get together. Gotta love one another right now" (Let's Get Together). I know this sounds a bit cliché, but this is the spirit James Rouse intended to embody in Columbia.

Being a product of Columbia doesn't end at the gates of this marvelous city. We have a responsibility to lead by example and share our experience in order to spread Columbia's message as far as possible. We are a testament to just how successful James Rouse's "grand social experiment" has been.

Ask yourself, "Have I helped even one person to become a more accepting and honorable human being?" "What more can I do to help the world see the value in embracing and honoring the diversity among us?" Let us stand together and make a promise to rise above closed-mindedness and oppression, and shine light on the path we have had the privilege to walk growing up in Columbia.

When faced with doubt from others who believe it cannot be done—that we cannot create community and cooperation among diverse peoples—share the story of Columbia and spread its message of hope with a resounding voice, "yes we can."

Columbia, Maryland has provided 50 years of evidence that people of diverse backgrounds and lifestyles truly can and do live together in peace and harmony.

Forever a Columbian,
Nancy Selig Amsden

APPENDIX 1:

Self-Honesty Reflection: A Prejudice Assessment

We have come a long way as a Nation since the 1960's when separation and racism inspired Rouse to take a stand and prove to the world that people, regardless of their differences, can live together in peace and harmony. However, we must never forget that the human tendency toward division and fear run deep and that prejudice, separatism, and racism still exist in our society—and sometimes even within our own hearts.

I would like to pose a few questions; some thoughts to ponder. I hope these questions will help you to look inside and "see" with eyes wide open what ways you may carry prejudice, even if you aren't aware of it. We are all a work-in-progress, and we have the ability to mold and shape the "me" we want to become.

In asking myself these questions, I found within myself things that I was not aware of. After becoming aware of my hidden thoughts and feelings, I have been able to shift my thinking in order to live in alignment with the core beliefs of unity and equality that have inspired my life and my passions.

Consider the following questions, honestly, in order to gain insight into your thoughts and feelings toward others and their differences. Remember that even those of us who grew up in a community whose mission was to encourage diversity still harbor biases and prejudice. These questions are not intended to point the finger or judge you for your beliefs, they're intended to help bring awareness to the prejudices that may exist within you, providing the opportunity to learn and grow.

Prejudice Assessment

• Do you think you are prejudice? (This can be tricky. Each of the following questions will help you dig deeper for answers.)

• Why do you think you are, or are not, prejudice?

• Have you ever made a decision about someone based solely on the way they look?

• Can an accent or speech patterns make you pass judgment before you really know someone?

• Have you ever made a statement that places a group of people into one behavioral category?

• Have you ever made a decision to do, or not do, something based solely on what you have been told about a certain neighborhood, town, city, country....?

• If you have children, have you ever said something to your children like, "We don't believe like they do, so you..." or "We don't want people to think that..." or how about, "If you do that, people will think you..."

• When describing someone, have you ever made the first trait you mention about them the color of their skin, their religion, their sexual orientation...?

Chances are you have answered "yes" to at least one of these questions. I know I have. And it is a normal, human condition to make decisions based on what we have been told, have experienced ourselves, or have been shown through actions or media influence.

The question is, "How can we all reduce our prejudices and biases?"

The Power of Conscious Description

I have made it a point in my life to change what adjectives I use when describing other people. For example, if you are describing a person at a party, consider saying something like, "the guy over there by the window with the blue shirt," instead of saying, "the black guy over there." There is nothing wrong with identifying someone with a physical trait, but is that physical trait the most important thing about them? Probably not. Many people often assume, when pointing someone out, that the only (or at least the best) way to describe them is by their "color." But by choosing to describe someone in a way that does not label them, you actually change how you view that person and how others around you will view them, too.

Another thing to watch out for is defining someone based on physical attributes or other classifications, to aid in identification, even when you're not trying to describe what they look like. For example, someone was speaking to me about an attorney they were working with. The first thing they said to describe this person was "This little Jewish guy." I did not know this man. Did his stature or religion make any difference to me? Did this description actually define the person? No, it did not. Another example: Someone was telling me about an experience of meeting a nice person in line at the grocery store. The first thing the person said about the encounter with this woman was, "This black lady...." Was the fact that she was black relevant? No, it was not.

We don't realize how much we label people. It is interesting that when describing someone different than themselves most people identify the other person based on their "race." Think about this... If you are white, how many times have you started a description with "That white girl..." Yet, have you ever started a description with "That black girl..."? To take it a step further, when describing or talking about someone, it is common practice to say something like "He was as black as black" or "That pasty white girl." Not only is the person's skin color an identifier, but further definition, typically not nice or necessary, is added. Listen to other conversations and how others refer to someone they are describing. Make mental notes and watch how just being aware can help you to "see" the world around you differently.

There is a great deal of value in those things that make us different. However, when labeling and describing others based on physical or cultural traits that are irrelevant or, worse, lead to false assumptions about them, the description is not for the purpose of emphasizing the value of their differences. Whether we mean to or not, describing people this way causes judgment and separation, not unity and appreciation for differences.

We can all do a better job at letting the individual qualities of a person characterize them, versus a description of what we see on the outside, or our opinion of what we think to be true about their ethnicity.

If we each continue to do everything we can — whether that means making choices to use words that honor instead of separate, instilling values of diversity and equality in our children, or spreading the message of hope and equality — together we will further advance the progress toward a society based on the values of love, peace, understanding, compassion and embracing the differences between people.

APPENDIX 2:

About the Author: Nancy Selig Amsden

Nancy Selig Amsden tells the story of her experience growing up in Columbia, Maryland—a planned community that was designed to promote diversity and inclusion. Nancy is an author, singer, and songwriter whose compositions and writings focus on cultural awareness, social justice and honoring the world around her.

Nancy has had a 30-year career in consumer advocacy and regulatory compliance, and has participated in diversity management, cultural awareness and corporate culture initiatives. Nancy has had articles published in Transformation Magazine and contributed a chapter in the book Transform Your Life, Book 2 (Transformation Publishing). Several of her songs and lyrics have been published and recorded by Stellar Voice Productions, Inc. Columbia was developed by James Rouse in the late 1960's and was ranked the #1 Place to Live in 2016 by Money Magazine.

Her book explores how this "utopian" environment impacted her life, as well as provides testimonials from others who have called Columbia home. She highlights what worked in this "grand social experiment," what we can learn from Columbia, and how people of diverse backgrounds and lifestyles truly can live together in peace and harmony.

Sharing her story has inspired within her a new mission; to

develop a diversity curriculum for children that would introduce schools, teachers and administrators to the importance of diversity management.

For questions, comments, to share your experience living in Columbia or to invite Nancy to visit your organization, contact nancyseligamsden@gmail.com.

APPENDIX 3:

Some of Columbia's Most Interesting Street Names

Airybrink Lane

Apple Blossom Ride

Balmy Dew Way

Bare Bush

Basket Ring Road

Beaverkill

Bendbough Court

Best Times Path

Black Star

Blitheaire Garth

Broken Lute

Broken Staff

Calm Sunset

Caterskill Court

Catfeet Court

Celestial Way

Chase Lions Way

Clear Smoke

Constant Course

Coon Hunt Court

Corncockle Court

Cowpath Road

Cradlerock Way

Crazy Quilt Court

Cricket Pass

Cross Fox Lane

Daring Prince Way

Deep Calm

Deep Smoke

Delphinium Court

Departed Sunset Lane

Distant Bugles Court

Dried Earth Blvd

Ducks Foot

Elffolk Terrace

Empty Song Road

Enchanted Solitude Place

Endymion Lane

Evensong Mews

Flamepool Way

Flight Feather

Forty Winks Way

Fox Grape Terrace

Frostwork Row

Fruitgift Place

Gallows Road

Gay Topaz

Gentle Folk

Gerfalcon Road

Glass Tumbler Path

Gleaming Sand Chase

Goldamber Garth

Good Hunters Ride

Greek Boy Place

Green Blade Garth

Grey Owl Garth

Hat Brim Terrace

Hazel Thicket Drive

Hermit Path

High Bench

Hobnail Court

Honey Laden Place

Honeycomb Gate

Hundred Drums Row

Indian Pipe Court

Iron Pen Place

Jacobs Ladder

Jamina Downs

Jeweled Hand Circle

Kilimanjaro Road

Kind Rain

King's Meade Way

Lacelike Row

Lady Bug Row

Lambskin Lane

Lame Beaver Court

Latchkey Row

Leafy Screen

Lilac Sea

Liquid Laughter Lane

Little Boots

Long Look Lane

Loveknot Place

Low Tide Pass

Madrigal Terrace

Majestic Days Way

Many Mile Mews

Marble Fawn Lane

Mellow Twilight Court

Melting Shadows Lane

Mickeys Pride

Midas Touch

Misty Arch Run

Moon Portrait Way

New Car Drive

Night Roost Court

Nodding Night Court

Oaken Door

Old Buggy Court

Old Romance Road

Ourtime Lane

Oven Bird Green

Painted Rock Road

Painted Yellow Gate

Paul Revere Ride

Pink Wood

Polished Stone

Possum court

Pressed Gentian

Prophecy Place

Quantrell Row

Quiet Night Ride

Raccoon Court

Rain Dream Hill

Rainbow Span

Red Cravat Court

Red Keel

Reedy Brook Lane

Resting Sea

Ripplestir Place

Rising Moon

Rocksparkle Row

Rushlight Path

Rustling Leaf

Rusty Rim

Same Song Square

Sandalfoot Way

Scarlet Petal

Sea Change

Sealed Message Road

Setting Star

Shadowmere Mews

Sharp Antler

Short Wheel Way

Silas Choice

Silent Bird Court

Silver Twine

Sixpence Circle

Slalom Way

Sleeping Dog Lane

Slender Sky

Snowy Reach

Solar Walk

Spelling Bee

Spinning Seed

Springing Step

Starsplit Lane

Stray Camel Way

Summer Rambo Court

Sylvan Dell

Talisman Lane

Tawny Bloom

Tender Mist Mews

The Bowl

The Mending Wall

Thelo Garth

Tilted Stone

Timesweep Lane

Tinker Round

Tolling Clock Way

Tower Top

Tufted Moss

Tunemaker Terrace

Twenty Year Chase

Twinedew Place

Two Ships Court

Velvet Path

Vollmerhausen Drive

Waiting Spring

Waking Dreams Knolls

Wandering Way

Wandering Way

Warmstone

Waveland Way

Wayover Way

Westering Sun

Wild Bees Lane

Wild Wing Way

Wind Dance Way

Wishing Bridge

Woven Moonbeam

Yellow Rush Pass

Made in the USA
Charleston, SC
15 October 2016